The Sharing Circle

Themes for Home and School Involvement

by Carol Spangler

Fearon Teacher Aids

Executive Editor: Jeri Cipriano

Editor: Susan Eddy

Illustration: Lydia Anderson

FEARON TEACHER AIDS
An Imprint of Modern Curriculum
A Division of Simon & Schuster
299 Jefferson Road, P.O. Box 480
Parsippany, NJ 07054-0480

ISBN: 0-86653-868-2

1 2 3 4 5 6 7 8 9   MAL   01 00 99 98 97 96

Table of Contents

INTRODUCTION

Children have always enjoyed bringing beloved objects from home to share with their classmates and teachers. Show-and-tell helps children develop their communication skills and links home and school. Sometimes, however, show-and-tell promotes envy and competition as children try to surpass each other with the latest "fad" toy.

As owner and director of Treebrook Preschool in Iowa City, Iowa, I decided to eliminate this problem by giving special importance to what we call our "sharing time" or "the sharing circle." I developed monthly themes for sharing time to give it a focus. I then developed each theme by reading picture books, sharing songs, and planning theme-related activities integrated into all areas of the curriculum.

The transition from an ordinary show-and-tell to a rich theme-sharing one was very successful. Children continue to be just as eager to share. Parents appreciate knowing the learning focus each month and having the opportunity to participate. Teachers, too, love the program for its spontaneity and flexibility.

SAMPLE MONTHLY THEMES

October: What Do People Do All Day?

In the middle of September, I send letters home explaining October's theme, its objectives, and suggestions for sharing. Children might bring a parent to school to demonstrate what he or she does at work. The class would see tools, machines, or uniforms associated with the job. In addition, children may learn why the job is important, what parts are enjoyable, and how the parent learned the skills for the job. Parents might arrange field trips to their places of work. Or children might share "prop boxes" of materials that suggest particular occupations. The class then uses the materials for dramatic play.

What sort of responses do we get? Generally, more than one-third of mothers and fathers visit our class. In one month, we met a dental hygienist, delicatessen worker, physician, artist, mother, midwife, pharmacist, car mechanic—among others. David's dad, a field geologist, showed us his field pack and contents (hammer, shovel, tape recorder, notebook and pen, and even some toilet paper). He showed fossils from Iowa quarries and gave each child a fossil and specimen bag as a souvenir. He discussed how he became interested in rocks and what he likes about his job. We extended the children's learning by having them sort fossils in various ways and they participated in a visualization exercise in which they imagined themselves as rocks in a stream. We read the story *Everyone Needs a Rock* by Byrd Baylor. Afterwards, we brainstormed different ways to use a rock. David's dad was one of many parents who stayed the whole morning and interacted with the children.

Ishi's mother related how she teaches dancers and singers proper body alignment and use of their bodies. She brought her dulcimer and sang folk songs from North Carolina. Peter's mother demonstrated her artistic abilities and read a favorite book, *A House Is a House for Me*, by Mary Ann Hoberman. Other parents arranged field trips. We visited a farm, a grocery store—even a bagel factory!

Children who chose to share "prop boxes" included Albert, who brought his train set and came outfitted like his great-grandpa, who worked for the railroad. Albert blew his whistle and we all sang, "I've Been Working on the Railroad." We listened to the book tape of *Train Song* by Diane Siebert and enjoyed the colorful pages of *Freight Train* by Donald Crews.

Kate, who wants to be a pet veterinarian someday, brought in her whole collection of stuffed animals. We determined whether each animal would be cared for by a pet vet, a zoo vet, or a farm vet. Kate shared a book about a cat needing surgery and dramatized the procedure.

Michael told us about houses he saw under construction on his way to school. He brought in a set of carpentry tools. During play time, children took turns hammering small nails and inserting screws into holes pre-drilled in a pine board. We sang "Johnny Works with One Hammer" and read *A Carpenter* by Douglas Florian.

Each October, children learn about many jobs, with each class engaged in different activities, depending on the interests and backgrounds of the children and their families.

February: Friendship Patchwork
Another kind of sharing is demonstrated through February's theme. Parents contribute four or five 6" x 6" (15 cm x 15 cm) patches of fabric. At sharing time, each child tells where the patches came from and talks about memories the particular fabrics evoke. After everyone shares, the squares are sewn together to make a patchwork quilt, a curtain, a pillow cover, or even a "remembrance skirt" for a teacher—whatever the children decide. Over the years, we have had samples of

clown outfits parents had made, pieces from baby bibs, sections of baby blankets, samples of curtains, and so on. Family members have been represented through scraps from a father's shirt or a mother's summer dress. We've even had pieces of a mother's high school prom dress and another's wedding gown!

Children identified strongly with the pieces of fabric they brought. As our fabric basket grew fuller, we sorted the squares in various ways (color, design, hue, texture). We read stories about friendship, such as *The Rag Coat* by Lauren Mills. Finally, the children chose to make a patchwork quilt, graciously sewn together by a talented parent. The children played on (and under) the quilt and pointed with pride to their own pieces of fabric. Parents, too, gathered around the quilt, shared stories, and marveled at the variety of contributions.

HOW THE PROGRAM IMPLEMENTS DEVELOPMENTALLY-APPROPRIATE PRACTICE

Monthly themes, such as the two examples just cited, are the conceptual organizers around which a developmentally-appropriate early childhood program is created. The themes are of intrinsic interest to children, yet broad enough for children to have many choices for sharing. Since the curriculum derives from the children themselves, the program is always relevant to their family backgrounds and cultures. Having children's sharing times evenly distributed over the month makes them feel especially valued because much attention is given to each sharing contribution. Children look forward to their special days and plan for them with their parents. Teachers can respond to the needs and interests of the children by adding new concepts and skills to what students bring from their own life experiences.

This spirit of mutual cooperation between parents and teachers greatly benefits children. Likewise, the program fosters positive social interaction and caring. Many of the themes involve group cooperation, recognition, and appreciation of individual differences.

HOW TO USE THE PROGRAM

Each child is assigned a special sharing day once a month. (Parents receive calendars indicating their child's day.) Children's sharing days are evenly distributed throughout the month, allowing for no more than three children to share on a particular day. Parents receive letters the preceding month describing the upcoming theme and offering ideas for sharing. The monthly theme is integrated into all areas of the curriculum, with special attention given to quality literature, art and music, math, science, and social studies. Experiences are provided that stimulate learning in all developmental areas—physical, social, emotional, and intellectual.

The teacher, as facilitator, introduces the theme, creates a stimulating environment, responds to children's interests, and provides experiences in which each child can succeed. Teachers can extend learning in a variety of creative ways and can use this curriculum in half- or full-day programs in any preschool, daycare, Head Start, kindergarten or early childhood setting. The themes work well for single or multi-age groups and there are many opportunities to learn from peers.

A WORD ABOUT CONTENTS AND ORGANIZATION

Since many children attend the same early childhood program for consecutive years (for example, at ages three and four), there are two years of monthly themes provided. Both sets start with September and end with May. In addition, there is one summer sharing theme.

Each monthly section includes objectives, a monthly commentary, two letters to parents (one for each year) that may be duplicated or used as models, suggestions for activities, such as arts and crafts ideas and cooking projects, and related songs and rhymes. Also included are bibliographies of poems and picture books related to each theme. It is hoped that this program becomes a framework to which teachers can add their own favorites and which, of course, can be the basis of quality sharing time for children, parents, and teachers. The letter on the following page is the one we send to all Treebrook Preschool parents at the beginning of each year.

Dear Family:

This year, we will give special importance to show-and-tell, or what we call our "sharing time." A different sharing theme each month lends a special focus and helps to create a stimulating environment for your child. We will expand your child's horizons by introducing new ideas, offering fresh challenges, and nurturing your child's development in all areas.

Every month, you will receive a letter describing the next month's theme and including suggestions for sharing time. We will also send a calendar indicating the day for which you should make special preparations. No more than three children will have their sharing time on a given day.

We would like each child to bring a piece of fresh fruit for snack every day. Besides providing excellent nutrition, we will use the fruit to help develop children's awareness of their five senses. On the last day of each month, children will slice their fruit, put the pieces into a big bowl, and mix them with everyone else's fruit to make "Friendship Fruit Salad." In the fall, children will enjoy using an old-fashioned apple corer/peeler/slicer. If anyone has a juicer to loan, it would be a treat to make fresh juice occasionally.

We welcome your presence and participation in our program. If you'd like to become involved, we offer many opportunities throughout the year. We believe you can make a significant contribution to our program as well as greatly benefit your child.

During each month, we will be developing a particular theme by reading picture books, learning songs, and engaging in a variety of theme-related activities. We look forward to your involvement with us this year. Together, we will have a lot of fun!

Sincerely,

Your Child's Teachers

8

DESCRIPTION OF MONTHLY SHARING THEMES: FIRST YEAR

SEPTEMBER: I AM THANKFUL EACH DAY

Objectives

- Children will gain greater self-awareness.
- Children and teachers will become better acquainted.
- A positive climate will be established early in the school year.

Children receive blank booklets with which to make personal books of things for which they feel thankful. Children may include drawings of favorite things and places, pictures from old magazines, family photographs, and so on. Classroom activities include making thank-you cards.

OCTOBER: AUTUMN DAYS

Objectives

- Children will become aware of changing seasons.
- Children will become more familiar with several fall holidays.

Children choose things to share that suggest the season of autumn. Possibilities include objects found on a nature walk, harvest fruits and vegetables, tools used for autumn tasks, a football or soccer ball, a jack-o'-lantern or Halloween costume, an autumn craft, such as a homemade mask, autumn flower bulbs, chrysanthemums, leaves, nuts, or information about "spooky" creatures, such as spiders, bats, and skeletons. Children might also share a seasonal poem or song, or tell about another October holiday, such as Succoth or Columbus Day. Visiting an apple orchard is a planned classroom outing.

NOVEMBER/DECEMBER: MY FAMILY TRADITIONS

Objectives

- Inter-generational relationships will be fostered.
- Children will learn about the values, heritage, culture, and traditions of their own families and others.
- Children will learn about past times.
- Children will learn to understand and accept diversity in families.

Children share something of their family's past. One possibility is to bring a grandparent to school for a visit. Alternatively, the child might

bring an old toy, quilt, or object that belonged to a parent or grandparent; children might share songs, games, stories, or fingerplays that a grandparent remembers from childhood. Children might tell how their ancestors came to this country, tell about a family tradition, share food samples from old family recipes, share old-fashioned crafts, tell about harvest festivals from their own culture, or tell how their family will observe Thanksgiving or their December holiday. Booklists include numerous books that celebrate our diversity.

JANUARY: TOYS ON PARADE

Objectives

- Children will share their toys.
- Children will learn to respect the possessions of others.

Instead of individual sharing times this month, special days are designated for these traditional toys: wind-up toys, teddy bears, balls, jack-in-the-boxes (or toys with springs), dolls, toys with wheels, and tops or toys that spin. Children have several opportunities to share during the month. Each special day lends itself to a fun classroom activity, such as singing "The Wheels on the Bus" and making macaroni-wheel collages.

FEBRUARY: FRIENDSHIP PATCHWORK

Objectives

- Children will learn to classify various fabrics according to color, design, and texture.
- Children will develop a sense of group unity.
- Children will take part in group decision making.
- Children will practice friendship skills.

Each child contributes four or five patches of fabric from home, cut into 6" x 6" (15 cm x 15 cm) squares. Children tell where their scraps came from. During the month, children may play with the scraps or sort them by color, design, and texture. After everyone has shared, fabric pieces are sewn into a patchwork quilt, a curtain, a pillow slip, or a "remembrance skirt" for a teacher.

MARCH: HATS, HATS, HATS

Objectives

- Children will increase their awareness of various occupations, seasons, and cultures.
- Children will take part in imaginative play.

10

Children may choose to bring in one or more occupational hats, or hats for different kinds of weather or sports. Alternatively, children might bring a spring bonnet, a whimsical hat, or a hat from another country. Pairs of children will make and decorate papier mâché hats.

APRIL: MOTHER GOOSE ON THE LOOSE

Objectives

- Children will build language skills through dramatization.
- Children will enjoy the rhythm of language through thematic rhymes.

Children select one or more Mother Goose rhymes to dramatize for the class, using any desired props. Children either recite the rhyme(s) or invite other children to guess them.

MAY: THE EARTH IS OUR MOTHER

Objectives

- A love and respect for nature will be fostered in children.
- Children will become more ecologically aware.
- Children will learn that they individually can have an impact on the environment.
- Children will learn about Native American harmony with nature through books and song.

Children bring in natural specimens, crafts using materials found in nature, objects made from natural or recycled materials, or posters that illustrate a way to save our resources. The class will go on a nature hike.

SUMMER (EACH YEAR): FARMER'S MARKET

Objectives

- Children's natural senses of wonder will be enhanced.
- Children will learn where many foods come from.
- Children will learn which vegetables grow under and which grow above the ground.
- Children will learn which parts of plants are edible.

DESCRIPTION OF MONTHLY SHARING THEMES: SECOND YEAR

SEPTEMBER: WISH UPON A STAR

Objectives

- Children and teachers will become better acquainted.
- Children will hear stories that foster self-acceptance.
- Children will understand and appreciate different kinds of wishes.

Children are given blank booklets to make into personal wish books. Children may express particular desires on each page. Drawings, photographs, or pictures from old catalogues and magazines may be used. Book covers may be specially decorated. Parents may facilitate the creative process by encouraging responses to such statements as:

If I could go anywhere, I would . . .
If I could have anything, I would . . .
If I could do anything, I would . . .
When I grow up, I wish to be a . . .

Parents record responses in their child's own words. For sharing time, children talk about their books. This month's classroom activity is a performance of the musical folktale, "The Little White Rabbit Who Wanted Red Wings."

OCTOBER: WHAT DO PEOPLE DO ALL DAY?

Objectives

- Children will build their awareness of various occupations.
- Children will learn to view job opportunities for men and women on an equal basis.
- Children will begin imitating some of the new skills they have observed from visiting adults.

Children might bring a parent to school to demonstrate what he or she does at work. The class would see tools, machines, or uniforms associated with the job. In addition, children learn why the job is important, what parts are enjoyable, and how the parent learned the skills for the job. Parents might arrange field trips to their places of work. Or children might share "prop boxes" of materials that suggest particular occupations. The class uses the materials for dramatic play.

NOVEMBER/DECEMBER: THE JOY OF GIVING

Objectives

- Children will think about various ways to express love and appreciation.
- Children will develop concern for those less fortunate.
- Children will consider the value of giving.

Children may share a present they have made for someone and describe how it was made, who it is for, and why that person is special. Throughout the months, children may bring in new or used toys in good condition to put under the classroom's "Giving Tree." The toys will be given to a hospital or shelter. Classroom activities include making simple presents, such as art calendars.

JANUARY: RING OUT THE OLD, RING IN THE NEW!

Objectives

- Children will build language skills as they learn about opposites.
- Children will gain exposure to the concept of *enduring value* as opposed to *fad.*

Children bring in two similar toys or objects—one old, the other new—to compare and contrast. The old and new toys will lead children to explore the concept of opposites. Classroom art activities include using contrasting textures and colors.

FEBRUARY: ANIMALS AS OUR FRIENDS

Objectives

- Children will learn about pet responsibility.
- Children will learn how birds and animals survive the winter.
- Children will learn compassion for animals.

Children may bring their pets for short visits. Children may tell how they are responsible for the pet and give information about its care. Alternatively, children may bring stuffed toys, drawings, or pictures of favorite animals. One classroom activity will be making edible valentines for birds.

MARCH: TICKLING OUR FUNNY BONES

Objectives

- Children will build language skills through the enjoyment of humor.
- Children will be encouraged to apply humor to a variety of craft projects.

Children bring comical toys, tell jokes, share nonsensical poems or amusing stories, show humorous pictures, or sing silly songs. Children will engage in unusual art activities, such as making mud paintings after reading *Piggy in the Puddle* by Charlotte Pomerantz.

APRIL: LITTLE THINGS

Objectives

- Children will begin to understand growth in nature and become aware of spring's newness.
- Children will expand their vocabularies by learning words that indicate smallness.
- Children will learn that smallness depends upon one's perspective.

Children may bring little treasures they like to collect, such as pebbles, rocks, or shells. Children might show garden seeds, insects, small pets or farm animals, baby brothers or sisters, or a special article of baby clothing. Miniature toys are another option. One classroom activity this month is planting seeds.

MAY: GOING PLACES

Objectives

- Children will learn about different kinds of transportation.
- Children will learn elements of geography and mapping.
- Children will learn about various kinds of vacations, such as going to a beach, going camping, or visiting a small town or city.
- Children will learn to tell stories in sequence.

Children share pictures, maps, and souvenirs from remembered vacations. Alternatively, children tell about their summer vacation plans. Parents might help children make photo-essay books of actual or imagined family trips or excursions. Classroom activities include outings around town.

September

First Year

I AM THANKFUL EACH DAY

Objectives

- Children will gain greater self-awareness.
- Children and teachers will become better acquainted.
- A positive climate will be established early in the school year.

Second Year

WISH UPON A STAR

Objectives

- Children and teachers will become better acquainted.
- Children will hear stories that foster self-acceptance.
- Children will understand and appreciate different kinds of wishes.

COMMENTARY

About Starting School

It is extremely important to help children make smooth transitions from home to school. Children vary greatly in the length of time they need to separate successfully. It is possible to minimize this period of adjustment in several ways. The key is to form a good relationship with each child's parents. Separation is difficult for parents too and they need to feel comfortable with the teacher.

Before school starts, it is helpful for teachers to visit each child's home and give parents a school handbook, a daily schedule, and a list of suggested books they might read to their child about starting school.

Another possibility is to arrange for small groups of children and parents to visit school before the year officially begins. Children play while parents and teachers visit with each other. When parents feel comfortable about leaving their children, a foundation will have been laid for a cooperative partnership between home and school.

Parents should be encouraged to stay with their children for the first day of school. This provides an opportunity for parents to meet each other and to see the daily routine. In this way, parent confidence in the teacher and the program is established.

The Sharing Circle is an opportune time for the children to get to know the teacher, the daily routine, and classroom expectations. The sharing themes, activities, and songs for this month will help children learn each other's names and feel special. It is reassuring for children to do familiar activities and songs at this time. Children will also feel most comfortable if the environment is calm and if they are encouraged to bring in a favorite cuddly toy during this transition period. After children have their special monthly sharing, their "thankful books" remain on view in the classroom so that everyone gets to know each other better.

In these small ways, children know that they are loved and respected as individuals. They can feel safe in their new environment. Learning how to separate gracefully can help children grow in competence and independence. It can prepare children for future separations that are a continual part of each person's life.

Teachers can help parents understand that parents are still the most important adults in their children's lives but that teachers and parents can be a mutual support system. A good link between home and school is important to establish. Refer to the bibliography on pages 32–34 for suggested reading for parents, children, and teachers regarding children and the beginning of their school career.

I AM THANKFUL EACH DAY
LETTER TO PARENTS

Dear Family:

In September, our theme is **I Am Thankful Each Day**. We will give you a blank booklet to help your child make his or her own "Thankful Book." Talk with your child about a few special times or special things he or she enjoys—feels glad or thankful for. Your child may wish to make drawings for the book or add special collage items. You might also furnish your child with some old catalogs or magazines in which to find desired pictures, or you might have family photos to share. For your child's sharing time, he or she may talk about each page. This special book will help acquaint us with your child and family.

We would also like to encourage an appreciation for all the good things upon this earth. Classroom activities will include reading books and poems about nature or wonder. We will promote joy and wonder by exploring color with watercolors. We will also engage in explorations of natural phenomena, such as making bubbles. Our five senses will be developed as we "explore" fruit. We will also practice saying please and thank you.

Sincerely,

Your Child's Teachers

WISH UPON A STAR
LETTER TO PARENTS

Dear Family:

In September, our theme is **Wish Upon a Star**. We will give each child a blank booklet to make into a personal wish book. Your child may express a particular desire on each page using drawings, photographs, or pictures cut from old catalogs and magazines. The book cover may be specially decorated. You can facilitate the creative process by encouraging a response to such leading statements as:

    If I could go anywhere, I would . . .
    If I could have anything, I would choose . . .
    If I could do anything, I would . . .
    When I grow up, I wish to be a . . .

Please record the responses in your child's own words. We will enjoy looking at the wish book during your child's sharing time—it will help us become better acquainted. We will read books this month that foster self-acceptance and demonstrate reasonable, unselfish kinds of wishes. The children will dramatize a musical version of the folk tale, "The Little Rabbit Who Wanted Red Wings."

               Sincerely,

               Your Child's Teachers

SUGGESTED ACTIVITIES FOR SEPTEMBER

COOKING PROJECTS

Ice Cream Social

Invite parents to attend an ice cream social on the first day of school. Everyone takes a turn at cranking an old-fashioned ice cream maker. This activity is definitely an ice-breaker! Parents and children all help with the cranking. Comparisons are made between the liquid mixture and the frozen ice cream. If time is limited, two or three quart-sized Donvier™ ice cream makers can be used instead. They are less messy; it takes only twenty minutes for the ice cream to freeze; the children can stir the mixture more easily.

Friendship Fruit Salad

It may become a tradition to make this on the last day of each month. Help children slice their snack fruit, put the pieces into a big bowl, and mix them with everyone else's fruit to make "Friendship Fruit Salad." In addition to being a cooperative venture, it gives children experience using a table knife to cut up food, mixing fruit together, and appreciating the combination of colors, shapes, and textures. You may wish to sprinkle a little grated coconut over the fruit salad or add some different fruits children have not brought in, such as kiwis or mangos. Provide small bowls and spoons and dig in. See page 231 for a related song to sing on Friendship Fruit Salad day.

ARTS & CRAFTS PROJECTS

Children will feel most comfortable using familiar materials, such as crayons, markers, and play dough, at the beginning of the school year. Use primary colors for painting activities. Introduce two colors at one time.

Circle Collages

Invite children to glue an arrangement of circles onto their papers. For paper-gluing projects, methyl cellulose blended with water is a strong, inexpensive, mess-free adhesive. Methyl cellulose can be obtained from a picture-framing or art supply store. Many school districts or area education agencies have production labs equipped with Ellison shape and letter presses for teachers to use. There are 1" (2.5 cm) and 4" (10 cm) Ellison circles as well as circle segments.

Harvest Paintings

If celebrating Succoth, children's paintings may decorate an outdoor hut.

Newspaper Hats

Help children make folded newspaper hats and decorate them with Ellison tiny shapes.

Pennants

Use the Ellison to cut out each child's initials. Display the initials on a work table and invite children to find and glue their initials onto pennants. Invite children to choose their favorite color from an assortment of Astrobright™ colors (available at copy centers) sliced diagonally into pennant shapes. Handles may be made from strips of matboard available as scraps from picture framers. The pennant-shaped paper is stapled or hot glued to the matboard strip.

ADDITIONAL IDEAS AND PROJECTS

Field Trip to an Orchard

Invite parents to accompany you and your students to see how apples and pumpkins are grown and discover the many varieties of apples, squash, and gourds. Perhaps you will see apple cider being pressed as well. Be sure to alert the orchard attendant that you are coming. Ask if children may each pick one or two apples to take back for snack or if they may each select a small pumpkin. Take a picture of the children with their apples or pumpkins to send as a thank you.

Pumpkins for Pediatrics

If you take your students on a pumpkin-picking field trip, consider having children decorate pumpkins to send to the pediatric wing of a local hospital. Children may use markers to make happy pumpkin faces and add festive party hats or other items. Invite one or two parent volunteers to deliver the pumpkins to the hospital.

I Am Thankful Each Day

Related Arts & Crafts Projects

Children's Books about Themselves

Share the book *Is This You?* by Ruth Krauss. Invite children to draw one page of their own book each day. Some things they might illustrate are their homes, their families, what they eat for breakfast, and so on. Use these topics for a circle time and story time theme each day. Motivate children with questions such as, *What does your favorite dinner look like?*

Paper Bag Puppets

Invite children to stuff lunch bags with newspaper. Then have them draw, cut, and paste on facial features. Yarn, wood shavings, or shredded office paper may be used for hair. Place small dowels in the bags and tape the openings shut. Puppets may be used when singing name songs as well as for a puppet theater.

Body Tracings

Outline children's bodies on sheets of butcher paper and invite children to decorate them with markers, paint, collage items, and pictures of favorite things. You may wish to read *The Important Book* by Margaret Wise Brown to encourage children to show important things about themselves.

Drawing with Motivational Starters

Cut pictures of children's clothing from old catalogs and glue them on pieces of drawing paper. Invite children to draw themselves "into" the clothes on the paper.

Thank You Cards

Encourage children to share people in their lives to whom they are thankful. Discuss with children special things these people have done. Then invite children to create thank you cards to send these special people. Give each child a 9" x 12" (22.5 cm x 30 cm) piece of colored construction paper folded in half. Help them write, "I am thankful for you!" and their names on the insides. Children may add appropriate illustrations on the fronts of the cards.

WISH UPON A STAR
RELATED ARTS & CRAFTS PROJECTS

Wishing Wand

Spray-paint wooden dowels gold and affix stars with a glue gun. You may wish to use the Ellison star shape cut from yellow posterboard. Decorate the wands with curling ribbon streamers. Invite children to add glitter to the stars. Wands may be used when singing "Star Light, Star Bright." Have children keep their wands lowered until they hear the word *star*. Each time children hear *star*, they raise their wands. Children may also wish to dance freely to music, holding their wands.

Wish Upon a Star Drawings

As a motivational starter, affix a star sticker to the center of a sheet of construction paper. Tape or glue a cellophane "window" over the star sticker to represent a child's bedroom window. Invite children to draw themselves into the pictures—looking out the window and wishing on a star. Encourage children to sprinkle "star dust" (glitter) on their papers or make their stars into a "falling stars" by adding star-dust trails. Children may also wish to draw their favorite dreams.

Wish Upon a Star

The Little Rabbit Who Wanted Red Wings
An Informal Parent Program

A musical folktale, "The Little Rabbit Who Wanted Red Wings," may be presented to parents at the end of the theme **Wish Upon a Star**. The teacher is the reader. To give all the children a character to play, consider letting more than one child play each part. All children may do the choral recitations. Stick puppets of all the characters may be made for children to use while portraying the various parts.

Characters

Rabbit
May wear a bunny costume or bunny ears. Holds a stuffed squirrel if available.

Duck (a non-speaking part)
May wear a yellow rain slicker, "duck" swim flippers, or a duckbill nose mask.

Porcupine (a non-speaking part)
May wear an oversized brown T-shirt and a picture of a porcupine. May wear a headband with chopsticks stuck around the band.

Groundhog
May wear an oversized brown T-shirt and a picture of a groundhog. Lives in a house by an oak tree with nuts strewn on the floor (make a little house with blocks; litter the floor with nuts).

Mammy
May wear an apron.

Squirrel
May wear an oversized brown T-shirt and a bushy tail with a wire support. The tree where squirrel lives may be a brown barrel with a cut-out round hole.

Red Bird
Purchase a red cardinal prop in the garden section of a store or silk flower shop. Rest it in a tree branch. The reader flies it down to the pond for a drink.

Additional Props
Wishing pond: Represented by blue netting placed near the tree branch.
Red wings: Use red netting over wire wings with over-the-shoulder elastic.
Bush: Represented by a green beanbag chair.
Carrot with a top
Nuts for the groundhog

The Little White Rabbit Who Wanted Red Wings

A Folk Tale
Music by Lucille Wood

Children: Everyone talks and everyone sings
Of the little white rabbit who wanted red wings.

Reader: Once there was a little white rabbit. He had two long, pink ears. He had two red eyes. He had four soft feet. But the little white rabbit was sad. He wanted to be different.

Children: He wished to be a squirrel instead.
He twinked his nose and scratched his head.
And this is what he said:

Rabbit:

I wish to be a big, gray squirrel and have a bush-y tail to curl.

Children: Old Mister Porcupine came by.
The little rabbit then did sigh:

Rabbit:

If I could have some bris-tles, Oh, I'd be so hap-py then, I know.

Children: Little Miss Puddle Duck with a yellow back
Paddled along saying, "Quack, quack, quack!"

Rabbit:

I wish I had some rub-bers red, and yel-low feath-ers on my head.

24

Reader: The little white rabbit wished and wished and wished. His mammy grew tired of his whining. One day Mister Groundhog said to the little white rabbit:

Groundhog: Go down to the wishing pond by the old oak tree.
Turn around three times and wish.
Your true wish you will see.

Reader: The little white rabbit went to the wishing pond. He saw a red bird drinking from the pond. He turned around three times and wished.

Rabbit:

A - round, a - round, and one, two, three, a red - bird I would like to be.

Reader: Then it happened! He began to feel something on his shoulders. It was wings coming through. The wings grew and grew. Soon they were full-grown red wings. The little white rabbit hopped home to show his mammy the red wings.

Mammy: What is this? What is this? Whatever can it be?
A rabbit with red wings cannot belong to me!

Reader: The little white rabbit with red wings had to go away and look for a place to sleep. His mammy did not know him. She would not let him sleep in his own little bed. He went to the squirrel's house.

Rabbit:

Oh, Mis - ter Squirrel please let me creep in - to your hole and go to sleep.

Squirrel: I do not know you. Go away!

Children: The little white rabbit with two red wings
Was sleepy as sleepy could be.
He came to the groundhog's house beneath
The friendly old oak tree.

Reader: Mister Groundhog let the little white rabbit with red wings sleep on his floor all night. But the floor was covered with nuts and they made the little rabbit's feet hurt. In the morning, the little white rabbit spread his red wings. He tried to fly, but he landed in a bush. He could not get out.

Rabbit:

Please, oh, please, won't you help me? For I am caught as you can see.

Groundhog: Did I hear somebody shout?

Rabbit:

Please, oh, please, won't you help me? For I am caught as you can see.

Reader: Mister Groundhog helped the little white rabbit with red wings out of the bush. The little white rabbit did not want his red wings any longer. He did not know what to do. But Mister Groundhog was very wise. He told the little white rabbit to count to ten down at the wishing pond.

Groundhog: Go down to the wishing pond and count to ten.
Turn around three times, and wish them off again.

Reader: The little white rabbit did just that.

Rabbit:

Tick -tack - tee,   tick - tack - tee, my   wings are gone and   now I'm free.

Children: Hippety-hop, hippety-hop.
Back to his mammy without a stop.
Hippety-hop, hippety-hop.
She gave him a nice green carrot top.

Reader: His mammy was SO glad to see him. And the little white rabbit never again wished to be anything different from what he was.

Children: Everyone talks and everyone sings
Of the little white rabbit who wanted red wings.

I Am Thankful Each Day

Related Songs

Favorite Things   African Folk Tune

Sa-rah loves choc'late ice cream,

Sa-rah loves choc'late ice cream.

Sa-rah, Sa-rah, Sa-rah, Sa-rah,

Sa-rah loves choc'late ice cream!

Invite children to take turns thinking of something they love. Sing verses in their honor. After everyone has had a turn, you may wish to sing a verse about something everybody loves! This song is an adaptation of the song "Everyone Loves a Saturday Night."

The world is so full of a number of things,
I'm sure we should all be as happy as kings.
> *– Robert Louis Stevenson*

Round about, round about
Hot apple pie.
My father loves apples
And so do I.
> *– Mother Goose*

I AM THANKFUL EACH DAY

RELATED SONGS

Mary Wore Her Red Dress **Traditional**

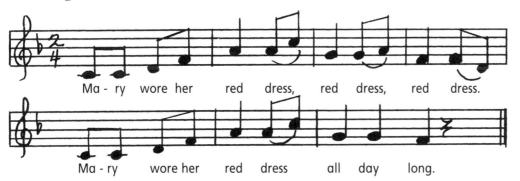

Ma-ry wore her red dress, red dress, red dress.

Ma-ry wore her red dress all day long.

I have ten little fingers
And they all belong to me.
I can make them do things.
Would you like to see?
I can shut them up tight
Or open them wide.
I can put them together
Or make them all hide.
I can make them jump high,
I can make them jump low,
I can fold them quietly
And hold them just so.

– Anonymous

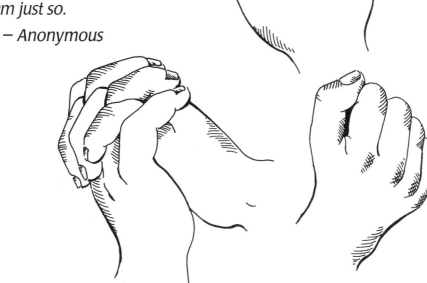

I Am Thankful Each Day

Related Songs

Paw Paw Patch Traditional

Where, oh where is good old John - ny?
(Sal - ly?)

Where, oh where is good old John - ny?

Where, oh where is good old John - ny?

Way down yon -der in the Paw Paw Patch.

2. Come on boys (girls) let's go find him (her) *(Sing 3 times)*
   Way down yonder in the Paw Paw Patch.

3. Come back Johnny (Sally) now we've found you *(Sing 3 times)*
   Way down yonder in the Paw Paw Patch.

4. Picking up paw paws, put them in your pocket *(Sing 3 times)*
   Way down yonder in the Paw Paw Patch.

Ring Around the Rosie Mother Goose

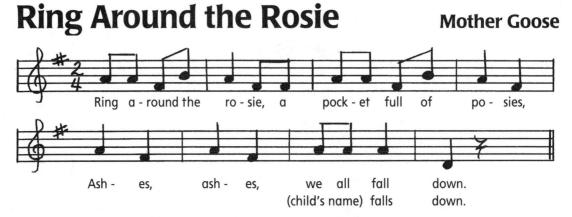

Ring a - round the ro - sie, a pock - et full of po - sies,

Ash - es, ash - es, we all fall down.
(child's name) falls down.

Playing familiar games is reassuring to children. Play the game the usual way a few times. Then invite each child to fall down in turn.

30

WISH UPON A STAR
RELATED SONG

Starlight, Starbright

Traditional

Star - light, star - bright, first star I see to - night.

Wish I may, wish I might, have the wish I wish to - night.

Game
Have children sit in a circle, passing a star wand on the steady beat.
Whoever has the wand at the end of the song may make a wish.
Children may gently keep the beat with finger cymbals or a triangle.

A Kite
I often sit and wish that I
Could be a kite up in the sky,
And ride upon the breeze and go
Whichever way I chanced to blow.
　　　　　　– Anonymous

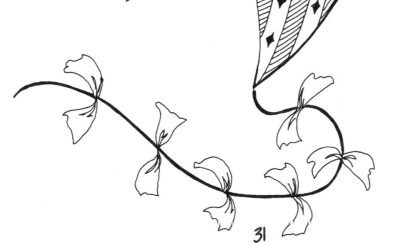

Touch blue,
Your wish will come true.
　　　　　　– Anonymous

31

BEGINNING SCHOOL

RELATED BOOKS FOR PARENTS AND TEACHERS

Ames, Louise Bates. *Don't Push Your Preschooler*. Harper & Row, 1974.

Babalon, Nancy. *Starting School: From Separation to Independence*. Teacher's College Press, 1985.

Baldwin, Rahima. *You Are Your Child's First Teacher*. Celestial Arts, 1989.

Brenner, Barbara. *The Preschool Handbook: Making the Most of Your Child's Education*. Pantheon Books, 1990.

Elkind, David. *The Hurried Child*. Alfred A. Knopf, 1984.

Elkind, David. *Miseducation: Preschoolers at Risk*. Alfred A. Knopf, 1987.

Elovson, Allana. *The Kindergarten Survival Handbook: The Before School Checklist and Guide for Parents*. Parent Education Resources, 1993.

Moore, Raymond and Dorothy. *Better Late Than Early*. Reader's Digest Press, 1975.

Moore, Raymond and Dorothy. *School Can Wait*. Brigham Young University Press, 1979.

Townsend-Butterworth, Diana. *Your Child's First School: A Handbook for Parents*. Walker, 1992.

Beginning School

Related Picture Books

Barkin, Carol. **I'd Rather Stay Home**. Raintree Children's Books, 1975.
Explores the fears and anxieties connected with leaving
home and starting school.

Breinburg, Petronella. **Shawn Goes to School**. Crowell, 1973.
A little boy adjusts to his first day at nursery school.

Cooney, Nancy. **Chatterbox Jamie**. G.P. Putnam's Sons, 1993.
Jamie enjoys all the activities at his nursery school but does
not talk until just the right time for him.

Glenn, Maggie. **Ruby to the Rescue**. G. P. Putnam's Sons, 1992.
Ruby the bear is taken to school by her owner and carries
out a plan to save two unwanted teddies in the playhouse.

Hoffman, Phyllis. **We Play**. Harper & Row, 1990.
A rhymed account of a child's fun-filled day at
nursery school.

Hurd, Edith. **Come with Me to Nursery School**. Coward-McCann, 1970.
A preschooler learns from photographs and brief text what
to expect in nursery school.

Kantrowitz, Mildred. **Willy Bear**. Parents' Magazine Press, 1976.
On the eve of his first day at school, a child projects some
of his uneasiness onto his teddy bear, Willy.

Kunhardt, Edith. **Red Day, Green Day**. Greenwillow Books, 1992.
Andrew and his classmates in Mrs. Halsey's kindergarten
class learn about colors in a unique way.

Moreman, Grace. **No, No, Natalie**. Childrens Press, 1973.
A rabbit describes a typical day with the children in
nursery school.

Oxenbury, Helen. *First Day of School*. Dutton, 1983.
A little girl is not looking forward to her first day at nursery school until she makes friends with another new girl.

Rockwell, Harlow. *My Nursery School*. Greenwillow Books, 1976.
A child discusses the various activities going on in nursery school.

Rogers, Fred. *Going to Daycare*. G. P. Putnam's Sons, 1985.
Describes the typical activities and feelings children can experience at a daycare center, including the fun, excitement, and apprehensions involved in being away from home.

Serfozo, Mary. *Benjamin Bigfoot*. Margaret K. McElderry Books, 1993.
Because he feels big when he wears his father's shoes, a little boy wants to wear them when he begins kindergarten.

Simon, Norma. *I'm Busy Too*. Albert Whitman, 1980.
Three preschoolers and their families have busy days at school and work.

Wells, Rosemary. *Timothy Goes to School*. Dial Books, 1981.
Timothy learns about being accepted and making friends during the first week of his first year at school.

I AM THANKFUL EACH DAY
RELATED PICTURE BOOKS

Austin, Virginia. *Say Please*. Candlewick Press, 1994.
Having heard the farm animals say "Please" with woofs, quacks, oinks and meows, Tom adopts the same noises when he asks his aunt to read a story.

Baer, Edith. *The Wonder of Hands*. Macmillan, 1992.
Describes, in verse accompanied by photographs, the many things hands can do.

Berger, Barbara. *Grandfather Twilight*. Philomel Books, 1984.
At the day's end, Grandfather Twilight walks in the forest to perform his evening task—bringing the miracle of night to the world.

Beskow, Elsa. *Pelle's New Suit*. Floris Books, 1989.
A little Swedish boy, his pet lamb, family, and friends all help make possible a new suit. All steps of the process are shown: shearing the wool, carding it, spinning, dying, weaving and sewing. Pelle expresses appreciation to all who help.

Brown, Marcia. *Once a Mouse*. Charles Scribner's Sons, 1961.
From ancient India comes this fable about humility and ingratitude.

Demi. *Demi's Secret Garden*. Henry Holt, 1993.
Excerpts from Walt Whitman, the Bible, Chinese nursery rhymes, and other literary sources accompany illustrations of such insects as the cricket, grasshopper, and pussmoth caterpillar.

Demi. *In the Eyes of the Cat*. Henry Holt, 1992.
A selection of Japanese nature poems (haiku) organized according to the seasons, and illustrated with paintings corresponding to the themes of the poems.

Denslow, Sharon. ***Night Owls***. Bradbury Press, 1990.
William and his aunt, both night owls, stay up late and experience the wonder of a midsummer night.

DePaola, Tomie. ***The Legend of the Bluebonnet***. G.P. Putnam's Sons, 1983.
A retelling of the Comanche Indian legend of how a little girl's sacrifice brought the flower called bluebonnet to Texas.

DePaola, Tomie. ***The Legend of the Indian Paintbrush***. G.P. Putnam's Sons, 1988.
Little Gopher follows his destiny, as revealed in a Dream-Vision, of becoming an artist for his people. He eventually is able to bring the colors of the sunset down to the earth.

Edwards, Michelle. ***Blessed Are You: Traditional Everyday Hebrew Prayers***. Lothrop, Lee & Shepard, 1993.
Prayers in transliterated Hebrew and English.

Field, Rachel. ***Prayer for a Child***. Macmillan, 1944.
An illustrated bedtime prayer which gives thanks for the many aspects of a child's world. Winner of the Caldecott Medal.

Gershator, David and Phillis. ***Bread Is for Eating***. Henry Holt, 1995.
Mamita explains how bread is created in a song sung in both English and Spanish, inspired by a Spanish song with the phrase "no tires el pan"—another way of saying "clean your plate."

Goble, Paul. ***I Sing for the Animals***. Macmillan, 1991.
Reflects on how we are all connected to everything in nature and how all things in nature relate to their Creator.

Hamanaka, Sheila. ***All the Colors of the Earth***. Morrow Books, 1994.
Reveals in verse that despite outward differences, children everywhere are essentially the same and all are lovable.

Highwater, Jamake. ***Songs for the Seasons***. Lothrop, Lee & Shepard, 1995.
Each season's song describes the changes that occur in nature as the year moves from summer through fall and winter to spring.

Hoban, Tana. ***Look Again!*** Greenwillow Books, 1971.
Hoban, Tana. ***Look! Look! Look!*** Greenwillow Books, 1988.
Photographs of familiar objects are first viewed through a cut-out hole, then in their entirety.

Marzollo, Jean. ***Sun Song***. HarperCollins, 1995.
Animals and plants respond to the sun's changing light over the course of a single day.

McDonnell, Janet. ***Thankfulness: What Is It?*** Childrens Press, 1988.
Describes the feeling we call thankfulness and the things that can make us thankful.

O'Neill, Mary. ***Hailstones and Halibut Bones***. Doubleday, 1951.
Twelve poems about different colors that can be heard, touched, and smelled as well as seen.

Rodandas, Kristina. ***Dragonfly's Tale***. Clarion Books, 1991.
After a poor harvest, two children regain the Corn Maidens' blessings for their people with the aid of a cornstalk toy, the dragonfly.

Roe, Eileen. ***All I Am***. Scholastic, 1990.
A little boy wonders about all he is, and all he will be.

Rossetti, Christina and Mary Teichman. *Color: A Poem*. HarperCollins, 1992.
> An introduction to colors and poetry for very young children.

Ryder, Joanne. *Mockingbird Morning*. Four Winds Press, 1989.
> Poems take the reader on an early morning walk to observe the animals of woods and water in happy solitude.

Related Poetry

de la Mare, Walter. "Here All We See." *Read-Aloud Rhymes for the Very Young*. Alfred A. Knopf, 1986.

Aldis, Dorothy. "Everybody Says" and "Here I Come." *All Together: A Child's Treasury of Verse*. G.P. Putnam's Sons, 1952.

Resources and References for Parents and Teachers

Carson, Rachel. *A Sense of Wonder*. Harper & Row, 1965.

Querido, Rene M. "The Development of Wonder, Gratitude, and Responsibility in the Growing Child." *Creativity in Education: The Waldorf Approach*. H.S. Dakin Co., 1982.

O'Neil, Gisela. "Gratitude, Love, Responsibility." *Waldorf Schools: Kindergarten and Early Grades*. Mercury Press, 1993.

WISH UPON A STAR

RELATED PICTURE BOOKS

Asch, Frank. **Moondance**. Scholastic, 1993.
Bear fulfills his dream of dancing with the moon.

Bailey, Carolyn. **The Little Rabbit Who Wanted Red Wings**. Platt & Munk, 1988.
A discontented little rabbit wishes for a pair of red wings, but the reaction of his mother and other animals convinces him that it is better just to be himself.

Bush, John. **The Fish Who Could Wish**. Kane/Miller, 1991.
A fish's wishes come true until the day he makes a foolish wish.

Caines, Jeannette. **I Need a Lunch Box**. Harper & Row, 1988.
A little boy yearns for a lunch box, even though he hasn't started school yet.

Caines, Jeannette. **Window Wishing**. Harper & Row, 1980.
A sister and brother spend a vacation with their fun and unconventional grandmother.

Carle, Eric. **The Mixed-Up Chameleon**. Crowell, 1984.
A bored chameleon wishes it could be more like all the other animals it sees, but soon decides it would rather just be itself. Cutouts along the edges of the pages display various animals and colors.

Carle, Eric. **The Very Quiet Cricket**. Philomel Books, 1990.
A very quiet cricket who wants to rub his wings together and make a sound as do so many other animals finally achieves his wish.

Carlstrom, Nancy. **Wishing at Dawn in Summer**. Little, Brown, 1993.
A brother and sister have different wishes during an early morning fishing trip.

Chess, Victoria. ***Poor Esme***. Holiday House, 1982.
> A lonely little girl wishes for a playmate, and her wish is
> finally granted in a way she never expected.

Cohen, Caron. ***The Mud Pony: A Traditional Skidi Pawnee Tale***.
Scholastic, 1988.
> A poor boy becomes a powerful leader when Mother Earth
> turns his mud pony into a real one, but after the pony turns
> back to mud, he must find his own strength.

Day, Alexandra and Ned Washington. ***When You Wish Upon a Star***.
Green Tiger Press, 1987.
> The 1940 song illustrated.

Fuchshuber, Annegert. ***The Wishing Hat***. Morrow, 1977.
> A man acquires a hat that grants his every wish.

Galdone, Paul. ***The Three Wishes***. Whittlesey, 1961.
> A fairy tale of a woodsman who gets three wishes from a
> fairy as a reward for sparing a giant oak tree.

Haas, Irene. ***The Maggie B.*** Atheneum, 1975.
> A little girl's wish to sail for a day on a boat named for her
> "with someone nice for company" comes true.

Hines, Anna. ***Moon's Wish***. Clarion Books, 1992.
> Molly is making a dandelion wish when she decides that
> the moon will make a wish with her, and as a result the
> wishes of all her family members come true.

Holder, Heidi. ***Carmine the Crow***. Farrar, Straus & Giroux, 1992.
> Carmine the Crow hears a cry for help and discovers a
> beautiful swan caught in a snare. He sets her free, and the
> swan gives Carmine a small box of stardust—for wishing
> on, she says. As he makes his way home, Carmine meets
> friends whose troubles seem more important than his own.

Jenkins-Pearce. ***Percy Short and Cuthbert***. Viking Penguin, 1990.
A very small hippo and his very large pelican friend discover that they really like the way they are during their adventures on the way to the Pingo-Pongo wish tree.

Kovalski, Maryann. ***Pizza for Breakfast***. Morrow Junior Books, 1990.
Frank and Zelda learn the folly of making wishes when they ask for more customers at their pizza restaurant.

Maris, Ron. ***I Wish I Could Fly***. Greenwillow Books, 1986.
Turtle wishes he could fly, dive, climb, and run like other animals but then he realizes something he can do that they can't.

Modesitt, Jeanne. ***Mama, If You Had a Wish***. Green Tiger Press, 1993.
If Little Bunny's mother could have one wish about her child, it would be to keep Little Bunny unchanged and loved by her.

Osborne, Mary. ***Moonhorse***. Alfred A. Knopf, 1991.
A winged horse takes a child on a wonderful night journey into outer space among the constellations.

Rogers, Fred. ***Wishes Don't Make Things Come True***. Random House, 1987.
A visit to the Neighborhood of Make-Believe shows us that wishes don't make things happen, people make things happen.

Rylant, Cynthia. ***The Dreamer***. Scholastic, 1993.
From his dreams an artist creates the earth, sky, trees, and all the creatures that dwell upon the planet.

Steig, William. ***Sylvester and the Magic Pebble***. Windmill Books, 1969.
In a moment of fright, Sylvester the donkey asks his magic pebble to turn him into a rock but then cannot hold the pebble to wish himself back to normal again.

Walter, Mildred. **Brother to the Wind**. Lothrop, Lee & Shepard, 1985.
With the help of Good Snake, a young African boy gets his dearest wish.

Watson, Pauline. **Wriggles, The Little Wishing Pig**. Seabury Press, 1978.
What's a little pig to do when his wish for a mouth like an alligator, wings like a pelican, and legs like a crane comes true?

Williams, Jay. **One Big Wish**. Macmillan, 1980.
Fred Butterspoon finds himself overwhelmed by a seemingly impossible situation when he is granted one big wish.

Zemach, Margot. **The Three Wishes: An Old Story**. Farrar, Straus & Giroux, 1986.
The traditional tale of the woodcutter and his wife who rescue an imp whose tail is caught under a fallen tree. Their reward of three wishes seems to be nothing but trouble and a string of sausages.

Zolotow, Charlotte. **William's Doll**. Harper & Row, 1972.
William's father gives him a basketball and a train but these do not make him want a doll less.

RELATED POETRY

Prelutsky, Jack, ed. **Read-Aloud Rhymes for the Very Young**. Alfred A. Knopf, 1986.
"If I Were Bigger Than Anyone" by Ruth Harnden, p. 78.
"Open House" by Aileen Fisher, p. 78.
"I'd Like to Be a Lighthouse" by Rachel Field, p. 78.
"The Wish" by Ann Friday, p. 29.
"If I Could Wish, I'd Be a Fish" by Dorothy Brown Thompson, p. 27.

Hoberman, Mary Ann. "I'd Like to Be a Kangaroo." **Yellow Butter, Purple Jelly, Red Jam, Black Bread**. Viking Press, 1981.

Li Po. "Firefly." **Sing a Song of Popcorn**. Scholastic, 1988.

OCTOBER

First Year

AUTUMN DAYS

Objectives

- Children will become aware of changing seasons.
- Children will become more familiar with several fall holidays.

Second Year

WHAT DO PEOPLE DO ALL DAY?

Objectives

- Children will build their awareness of various occupations.
- Children will learn to view job opportunities for men and women on an equal basis.

COMMENTARY

Children's Fears and Halloween Celebrations

At three-and-a-half to four years old, many children wake up in the night with nightmares. Fears are on the rise. At four, children are still quite fearful. Since they have such vivid imaginations at this age, they can be frightened by such things as monsters, witches, and ghosts. When children are five, they are better at verbalizing their fears and anxieties. But many children of this age are afraid of the dark, thunderstorms, and sirens. Between the ages of five and six, children may also fear heights, dogs, and death. It is often still hard for children of five or six to distinguish fantasy from reality. However, children are more able to spontaneously verbalize what is troubling them.[1]

Young children's fears are a reason for celebrating Halloween with a light touch. It is also important to discuss fears with children and to read stories about children who conquer fears. Pretend play is a healthy way for children to deal with their fears and to gain a sense of mastery over the unknown.

With the theme **Autumn Fun**, Halloween might focus on pumpkins, jack-o'-lanterns, and scarecrows. Children might enjoy making "leaf monster" masks, in which they glue dried leaves to cake liners with holes cut out for the eyes and tongue-depressor handles. Display masks, which are not worn, are another alternative. Children enjoy making the masks yet do not have to see them on each other.

Children again avoid the traditional Halloween costumes with the theme **What Do People Do All Day?** They may come to school dressed as particular workers, such as firefighters, police officers, carpenters, doctors, dancers, or farmers. Alternative Halloween celebrations are also recommended for children in primary grades. Interesting masks can be made using a facial form and plaster gauze.

---

[1]Caplan, Theresa and Frank. *The Early Childhood Years: The 2 to 6 Year Old*. Putnam, 1983.

AUTUMN DAYS
LETTER TO PARENTS

Dear Family:

In October, our theme is **Autumn Days**. The activities this month will help your child build an awareness of changing seasons. Your child may choose something to share that suggests the season of autumn. Some possibilities are:

- Objects from nature that your child finds on a fall walk.
- Products from your harvest fruit and vegetables.
- Tools your child uses to help with autumnal tasks, such as a rake or hand spade.
- A football or soccer ball your child plays with.
- Your child's jack-o'-lantern or Halloween costume.
- An autumnal art or craft project, such as a homemade mask.
- Flower bulbs your child will plant in autumn.
- Chrysanthemums from your garden.
- Autumnal collections to sort or display, such as leaves or nuts.
- Information and pictures about "spooky" creatures, such as spiders, bats, or skeletons.
- A seasonal poem or song your child has learned.
- Information about other October holidays that interest your child, such as Succoth or Columbus Day.

Sincerely,

Your Child's Teachers

45

WHAT DO PEOPLE DO ALL DAY?

LETTER TO PARENTS

Dear Family:

In October, our theme is **What Do People Do All Day?** We will be talking with children about jobs. We might ask them what jobs they would like to have when they grow up. We might inquire: Why does this job interest you? Why do you think you would be good at it? How would you help other people in your community by doing this job? We hope to build children's awareness of various occupations. We will foster the view that there are equal job opportunities for both men and women. Only one or two children will be scheduled to share each day. If you tell us in advance what your child expects to share, we will try to extend the learning by relating it to some books and activities. Here are three possibilities for sharing.

- You can come to talk or demonstrate what you do at work. We would like to see the tools needed in your job and a special uniform, if you have one. We would like to hear why your job is important, what things you enjoy about it and, how you learned to do it.
- You can arrange a field trip for the children to your place of work.
- Your child can share a prop box of materials that suggest a particular occupation. The class could explore the materials and, if you are willing, they may use them for dramatic play. Some ideas for prop boxes are included with this letter. For our Halloween party, we would like children to come dressed as people employed in certain jobs, such as firefighters, police officers, carpenters, doctors, dancers, or farmers.

Sincerely,

Your Child's Teachers

46

POSSIBILITIES FOR PROP BOXES

It would be enjoyable for children to have boxes of things from the real world to play with. A partial list of workers and possible tools or props is listed below. You may often obtain some of these materials by telling a business owner the purpose of the visit and asking for donated materials. A related picture book is also suggested.

Auto Mechanic: flashlight; keys on a ring; hat with visor; clean motor parts, such as spark plugs, filters, carburetors, cable sets, and gears; tools, such as hammers, pliers, screwdriver; oil funnel; empty oil cans; wiring; windshield wipers; rags; old shirts; gloves; automobile supply catalogues.
   An Auto Mechanic by Douglas Florian.

Barber/Beautician: mirror, brush, comb, hairpins, scissors (with blades taped), curlers, hairnet, dryer, tool and brush for shaving, towel, large bib, "beauty magazines," empty shampoo bottles, plastic basin, emery boards, play money.
   My Barber by Anne Rockwell.

Doctor: adhesive bandages, stethoscope, cotton balls, eye dropper, tongue depressors, plastic squeeze bottle, "prescription" pad, cloth bandages, toy hypodermic needle, hot water bottle, mask, gloves.
   My Doctor by Anne Rockwell.

Grocery Store Worker: play money, empty food packages, grocery bags, cash register, apron, coupons, name tag.
   The Supermarket by Charlie Fann.

Post Office Worker/Mail Carrier: mail bag (large tote bag), gummed labels or stickers for stamps, old circulars and magazines, small scale for weighing letters; brown paper and tape (to wrap packages), rubber stamp and pad, mail hat.
   Post Office Book by Gail Gibbons.

Electrician: electrical switches, wire, flashlight or trouble light, screwdriver, pliers, safety goggles.
   Building a House by Byron Barton.

Forest Ranger: canteen, flashlight, rope, mosquito netting, tent, knapsack, food supplies, nature guidebooks, small logs, binoculars.
   Ranger Rick magazines.

Suggested Activities for October

Cooking Projects

Have each child bring an apple to school. Invite children to explore the outside and inside of their apples using all five senses (see page 228). Children may also use an old-fashioned apple peeler/corer/slicer. Slices may be dried in a slow oven or dehydrator.

Have each child bring an orange to school. Encourage children to explore the outside and inside of their oranges using all five senses. Oranges may be decorated using bits of black paper and white glue to make jack-o'-lantern faces.

Discuss ways of preserving food from a fall harvest.

Arts & Crafts Projects

Halloween Masks
Cut two holes for eyes in a round cakeliner. A tongue depressor may be used for a handle. Encourage children to paint and decorate the masks with yarn, curling ribbon, glitter, sequins, stars, and stickers. Older children may make masks using foil-covered facial forms and plastergauze (ordered from an art supply store).

"Wild Things" Paintings
Glue a 4" (10 cm) colored circle (Ellison shape) to a sheet of drawing paper. Encourage children to use circles as starters to turn into their wild things. When the paintings dry, they may glue on hair or other features with wood shavings, shredded office paper, pieces of yarn, or buttons.

Paper Jack-o'-Lanterns
Give children pumpkin shapes cut from orange construction paper or have children cut out the shapes themselves from orange cardstock. Invite children to cut small shapes from black construction paper and glue them on for facial features.

Carbon Paper Prints
Give each child a piece of orange Astrobright™ paper and a half-sheet of carbon paper. Show children how to cut the carbon paper into the shapes they like and place them on their orange paper, shiny side down. (Shapes may overlap.) When children are pleased with their arrangements, carefully move the papers to the ironing board. Cover

the design with a protective sheet of paper and iron. Children reveal their designs by peeling off the carbon paper.

Paper Collages
Invite children to make arrangements of orange and yellow shapes torn or cut from construction paper on black backgrounds.

Scarecrows
Children may work together to stuff a shirt and pants with hay and create a face on a burlap bag. Help children assemble their scarecrow and invite them to add a hat, belt, and workboots.

ADDITIONAL GAMES AND ACTIVITIES

Cooperative Musical Chairs
Instead of putting children out of the game when the music stops, everyone must sit on fewer and fewer chairs until there is a big pile-up of children. The game ends when not all the children can "sit."

"Wild Thing" Shadow Dance
After reading *Where the Wild Things Are* by Maurice Sendak, invite children to dance behind a sheet hung in a corner of the classroom. Use an overhead projector to create shadows.

Haunted House
Rearrange the classroom to suit the purpose. Furniture may be draped with sheets and the room darkened. Add artificial cobwebs. Have children make their own tape of scary sounds to play while they crawl through their "haunted house."

Squirrels in the Trees Game
Children form groups of three. Two children join hands to form a tree. The third child is the "squirrel" in the center of the tree. A few children are extra squirrels without trees. When the teacher calls, "Run squirrels!" all the "trees" raise their arms while the squirrels attempt to relocate to another tree. Other motor skills, such as hopping, skipping, or tiptoeing, may be used in place of running.

Day at a Nature Park
Invite parents to participate in the day's activities. Play singing games, such as "Hop, Old Squirrel." Take a short hike and then read a story, such as *Chipmunk Song* by Joanne Ryder. Do a nature art project, such as leaf rubbings, or gather items for collages. Be sure to pack snacks!

AUTUMN DAYS

RELATED ARTS & CRAFTS PROJECTS

Leaf Rubbings
Have children bring some fresh-fallen leaves to school. Show children how to place paper on top of the vein sides of leaves and rub with the side of a red, orange, brown, or yellow crayon. Help them create pleasing arrangements with their rubbings.

Leaf-Stenciled T-Shirts
Ink a brayer (hard inking roller) and roll it over the vein side of a leaf. Place the leaf ink-side down on a T-shirt and roll with a non-inked brayer to transfer the design. Repeat as often as you like, using different ink colors.

Autumn Trees
Give children strips of black paper to glue onto sheets of sky blue construction paper to make tree trunks and branches. Have them gently dab small sponges or cotton swabs dipped in tempera on the branches and around the base of the trees to suggest autumn leaves. Alternatively, children may tape or glue fallen leaves they have collected.

Fall Collages
Use earth-toned wallpaper scraps, acorn caps, little pine cones, yarn bits, buttons in autumn colors, bits of burlap, and dried weeds. Earth-toned matboard from a picture-framing business makes a firm base. 3-D collages may be made using baker's clay platforms on which children may arrange fall collections.

Scarecrow Painting
Outline a scarecrow on a long sheet of butcher paper and place it on the floor. Invite children to paint the scarecrow and add yarn hair, bits of burlap, buttons, and other details when the paint is dry. Hang the scarecrow on the door.

WHAT DO PEOPLE DO ALL DAY?
RELATED ARTS & CRAFTS PROJECTS

Community Helper Drawings
As a motivational starter, show children a drawing of a particular occupational hat. Discuss what the person wearing that hat might do on the job. Invite children to choose from a wide selection of hats to begin their own drawings.

When I Grow Up
Ask children what kind of work they would like to do when they grow up. You might ask, *Why does this job interest you? Why do you think you would be good at it? How would you help other people in your community by doing this job?* Invite children to draw themselves at work on the job.

Smile Montage
Make a smile montage as a group project. Have children bring in magazine pictures of smiles—all ages and colors of people. Children may add some illustrated smiles as well. A toothbrush and tooth (Ellison shapes) may be glued to the center of the picture.

51

Hop, Old Squirrel

Virginia Folk Song

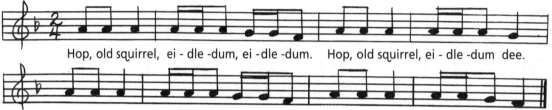

Hop, old squirrel, ei - dle -dum, ei -dle -dum.   Hop, old squirrel, ei - dle -dum dee.

Hop, old squirrel, ei - dle -dum, ei - dle -dum.   Hop, old squirrel,   ei - dle -dum dee.

Game

A hide-and-seek game may be improvised using the words, "Hide, old squirrel," then "Hunt for the squirrel." What else can the squirrel do? Alternatively, one-half of the children may hop on "Hop, old squirrel" while the other half hops on "eidledum, eidledum."

The Squirrel

Whisky, frisky
Hippity hop,
Up he goes
To the treetop!
Whirly, twirly,
Round and round,
Down he scampers
To the ground.
Furly, curly,
What a tail!
Tall as a feather,
Broad as a sail!
Where's his supper?
In the shell,
Snappity, crackity,
Out it fell!

– Anonymous

AUTUMN DAYS

RELATED SONGS

Let Us Chase the Squirrel
Traditional

Let us chase the squirrel, up the hick'-ry, down the hick'-ry,

Let us chase the squirrel, up the hick'-ry tree.

Apple Tree, Apple Tree
Traditional

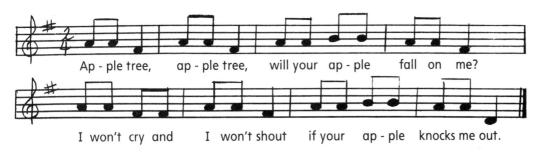

Ap-ple tree, ap-ple tree, will your ap-ple fall on me?

I won't cry and I won't shout if your ap-ple knocks me out.

Game

Children sit in a circle. An apple is passed around on the beat as the song is sung. Whoever has the apple at the word *out* sits out of the game. The game continues until just one child is left .

The boughs do shake and the bells do ring
So merrily comes our harvest in,
Our harvest in, our harvest in,
So merrily comes our harvest in.

We've plowed, we've sowed,
We've reaped, we've mowed,
We've got our harvest in.
                    – Anonymous

WHAT DO PEOPLE DO ALL DAY?

A Wishing Song   Traditional Song, Adapted

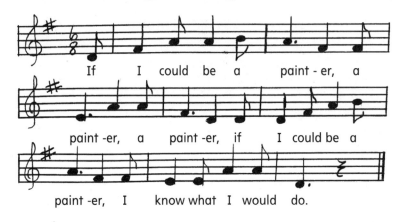

If I could be a paint-er, a

paint-er, a paint-er, if I could be a

paint-er, I know what I would do.

Action

Children take turns thinking what they would like to be
when grown up. Their choices replace the word *painter* in
the song. Children demonstrate an action that would
represent that career as they sing the new verse.

FEATURED BOOK

Rockwell, Anne. ***When We Grow Up***.
Dutton, 1981.

Contains pictures of children
demonstrating various jobs they
wish to have when they grow up.

RELATED SONGS

I've Been Working on the Railroad

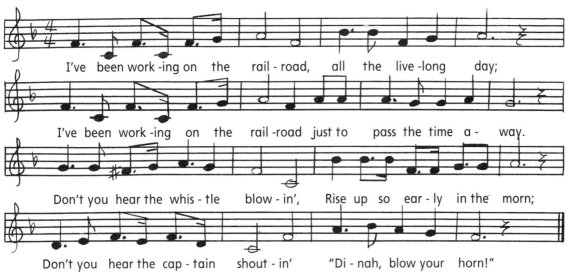

I've been work-ing on the rail-road, all the live-long day;

I've been work-ing on the rail-road just to pass the time a - way.

Don't you hear the whis - tle blow - in', Rise up so ear - ly in the morn;

Don't you hear the cap - tain shout - in' "Di - nah, blow your horn!"

Johnny Works with One Hammer

Traditional

John -ny works with one ham -mer, one ham - mer, one ham -mer,

John -ny works with one ham -mer, Now he works with two.

Action

Begin song by pounding with fist to a steady beat on one knee.
Continue singing the song with additional "hammers" added. Two
hammers: Use other fist to pound other knee. Three hammers:
Add one foot, tapping the floor. Four hammers: Add other foot.
Five hammers: Move head up and down. At the end of the verse,
"Johnny works with five hammers . . ." sing, "Now he falls asleep."
Sing it slowly and quietly while resting heads on hands.

RELATED SONGS

The Muffin Man

Traditional

Oh, do you know the muf - fin man, the muf -fin man, the muf -fin man; oh do you know the muf - fin man who lives in Dru - ry Lane?

2. Oh yes, I know the muffin man, the muffin man, the muffin man.
   Oh yes, I know the muffin man who lives in Drury Lane.
   (Besides "muffin man," children may name other community helpers.)

Game

Children stand in a circle. One blindfolded child stands in the center holding a rolled newspaper. The children circle around the blindfolded child as they sing. At the end of the first verse, the child touches someone with the rolled newspaper. That child sings the second verse (Oh yes, I know . . .). If the blindfolded child can guess who it is, they change places. Otherwise, the first verse is sung again, and another child is touched.

Tinker, Tailor

Tink - er, tai - lor, sol - dier, sai - lor, rich man, poor man, beg -gar -man, thief.

Game

One child walks around the outside of the circle, holding a purse and tapping the head of each child he or she passes by. The child whose head is tapped on the word *thief* gets up and chases the first child around the circle, trying to grab the purse before the first child gets back into the empty space.

HALLOWEEN OR JUST A BIT SCARY
RELATED PICTURE BOOKS

Brown, Marc. *Witches Four*. Parent's Magazine Press, 1980.
Four witches discover their lost magic hats have been turned into houses by four homeless cats.

Brown, Ruth. *A Dark, Dark Tale*. Dial Books, 1981.
Journeying through a dark, dark house, a black cat surprises the only inhabitant of the abandoned residence.

Bunting, Eve. *Scary, Scary Halloween*. Ticknor & Fields, 1986.
A band of trick-or-treaters and a mother cat and her kittens spend a very scary Halloween.

Delaney, A. *The Gunnywolf*. Harper & Row, 1988.
A little girl wanders into the woods to pick flowers and meets the dreaded Gunnywolf.

Galdone, Paul. *The Teeny-Tiny Woman: A Ghost Story*. Clarion Books, 1984.
Retells the tale of the teeny-tiny woman who finds a teeny-tiny bone in a churchyard and puts it away in her cupboard before she goes to sleep.

Goss, Janet and Jerome Harste. *It Didn't Frighten Me*. Willowisp Press, 1985.
The unusual colorful creatures a child sees each night after the lights go out don't frighten him, but an ordinary brown owl does.

Hutchins, Pat. *The Very Worst Monster*. Greenwillow Books, 1985.
Hazel sets out to prove that she, not her baby brother, is the worst monster anywhere.

Johnston, Tony. *Goblin Walk*. G.P. Putnam's Sons, 1991.
A little goblin has a series of frightening experiences while walking through the woods to his grandmother's house.

Ross, Tony. *I'm Coming to Get You*. Dial Books, 1984.
> After eating all the planets in outer space, a horrible monster gets a big surprise when it comes to Earth and tries to capture a little boy.

Seeger, Pete. *Abiyoyo*. Macmillan, 1986.
> Banished from the town for making mischief, a little boy and his father are welcomed back when they find a way to make the dreaded giant Abiyoyo disappear.

Sendak, Maurice. *Where the Wild Things Are*. Harper & Row, 1963.
> A naughty little boy, sent to bed without his supper, sails to the land of the wild things where he becomes their king.

Williams, Linda. *The Little Old Lady Who Was Not Afraid of Anything*. Crowell, 1986.
> A little old lady who is not afraid of anything must deal with a pumpkin head, a tall black hat, and other spooky objects that follow her through the dark woods.

RELATED POEMS

Prelutsky, Jack, ed. *Read-Aloud Rhymes for the Very Young*. Alfred A. Knopf, 1986.
> "Skeleton Parade" by Jack Prelutsky, p. 49.
> "On Halloween" by Aileen Fisher, p. 49.
> "Bedtime Story" by Lilian Moore, p. 49.

Bennett, Rowena. "The Witch of Willowby Wood." *Sing a Song of Popcorn*. Scholastic, 1988.

Flannelboard Pumpkin Rhyme
> *Five little pumpkins sitting on a gate,*
> *The first one said, "Oh my, it's getting late."*
> *The second one said, "Let's have some fun."*
> *The third one said, "Let's run and run and run."*
> *The fourth one said, "Now is our chance,"*
> *The fifth one said, "Let's do a spooky dance!"*
> *When "Whooo" went the wind and out went the light,*
> *And away rode the witch on Halloween night.*

AUTUMN DAYS

RELATED PICTURE BOOKS

Buscaglia, Leo. ***The Fall of Freddie the Leaf: A Story of Life for All***.
Holt, Rinehart & Winston, 1982.
> As Freddie experiences the changing seasons, along with
> his companion leaves, he learns about the delicate balance
> between life and death.

Ehlert, Lois. ***Red Leaf, Yellow Leaf***. Harcourt Brace Jovanovich, 1991.
> A child describes the growth of a maple tree from seed to
> sapling.

Gibbons, Gail. ***The Seasons of Arnold's Apple Tree***. Harcourt Brace
Jovanovich, 1984.
> As the seasons pass, Arnold enjoys a variety of activities as
> a result of his apple tree. Includes a recipe for apple pie and
> a description of how an apple cider press works.

Good, Elaine. ***Fall Is Here! I Love It!*** Good Books, 1990.
> A young child enjoys the sights, colors, tastes, and smells as
> fall comes to the family farm.

Hirschi, Ron. ***Harvest Song***. Cobblehill Books, 1991.
> A little girl and her grandmother share many activities
> together.

King, Elizabeth. ***The Pumpkin Patch***. Dutton Children's Books, 1990.
> Text and photographs describe the activities in a pumpkin
> patch as pink-colored seeds become fat pumpkins, ready to
> be carved into jack-o'-lanterns.

Knutson, Kimberley. ***Ska-tat!*** Macmillan, 1993.
> Children describe playing in the colorful, scratchy leaves as
> they fall from the trees.

Lewis, Tracey. ***Where Do All the Birds Go?*** Dutton, 1988.
> Tells where the birds, tortoises, squirrels, mice, fish, horses,
> and people go when it gets cold.

Lionni, Leo. ***Frederick***. Pantheon Books, 1967.
Frederick the field mouse sat on the old stone wall while his four brothers gathered food for the approaching winter days. The other mice felt that Frederick was not doing his share of the work, but when the food ran out, Frederick saved the day with what he had gathered.

Rockwell, Anne. ***Apples and Pumpkins***. Macmillan, 1989.
In preparation for Halloween night, a family visits Mr. Comstock's farm to pick apples and pumpkins.

Ryder, Joanne. ***Chipmunk Song***. Lodestar Books, 1987.
A lyrical description of a chipmunk as it goes about its activities in late summer, prepares for winter, and settles in until spring.

Slawson, Michele Benoit. ***Apple Picking Time***. Crown Publishing, 1994.
A young girl and her family spend a fall day picking apples with others from their small town.

Testa, Fulvio. ***Leaves***. Harper & Row, 1983.
Leaves in autumn drop to the ground but their adventures do not end there.

Wheeler, Cindy. ***Marmalade's Yellow Leaf***. Alfred A. Knopf, 1982.
Marmalade, a cat, causes a commotion when he tries to retrieve a particular yellow leaf.

Wildsmith, Brian. ***Squirrels***. Oxford University Press, 1974.
Text and watercolor illustrations describe the characteristics and habits of squirrels throughout the year.

WHAT DO PEOPLE DO ALL DAY?
RELATED PICTURE BOOKS

Alda, Arlene. ***Sonya's Mommy Works***. Little Simon, 1982.
> With Sonya's mother working, Sonya has adjustments to make, not all of which are easy.

Asbjornsen, Peter. ***The Man Who Kept House***. Margaret K. McElderry Books, 1992.
> Convinced that his work in the field is harder than his wife's work at home, a farmer trades places with her for the day.

Barton, Byron. ***Bones, Bones, Dinosaur Bones***. Crowell, 1990.
> A cast of characters looks for, finds, and assembles some dinosaur bones.

Barton, Byron. ***Building a House***. Greenwillow Books, 1981.
> Briefly describes the steps in building a house.

Barton, Byron. ***I Want to Be an Astronaut***. Crowell, 1988.
> A young child thinks about what it would be like to be an astronaut and go out on a mission into space.

Brown, David. ***Someone Always Needs a Policeman***. Simon & Schuster, 1972.
> Briefly relates some of the reasons policemen are so busy and why it's good to have them around.

English, Betty. ***Women at Their Work***. Dial Books, 1988.
> Twenty-one women, including a jockey, an orchestra conductor, a radio interviewer, a chemist, a firefighter, a judge, a carpenter, and a rabbi, briefly discuss their work.

Florian, Douglas. ***A Carpenter***. Greenwillow Books, 1991.
> A simple description of what a carpenter does.

Florian, Douglas. ***A Potter***. Greenwillow Books, 1991.
> Illustrates what a potter does with clay.

Florian, Douglas. *An Auto Mechanic*. Greenwillow Books, 1991.
Simple text and illustrations introduce the daily work of an auto mechanic.

Gibbons, Gail. *Fire! Fire!* Crowell, 1984.
Shows firefighters fighting fires in the city, in the country, in the forest, and on the waterfront.

Gibbons, Gail. *Farming*. Holiday House, 1988.
An introduction, in simple text and illustrations, to farming and the work done on a farm throughout the seasons.

Gibbons, Gail. *The Post Office Book: Mail and How It Moves*. Crowell, 1982.
A step-by-step description of what happens to mail from the time it is deposited in the mailbox to its arrival at its destination. Also includes brief historical facts about mail service in the United States.

Hazen, Barbara. *Mommy's Office*. New York: Atheneum, 1992.
Emily accompanies Mommy downtown to see where she works.

Henderson, Kathy. *In the Middle of the Night*. Macmillan, 1992.
During the night while almost everyone is asleep, cleaners, bakers, astronomers, nurses, doctors and many others carry on with their work.

Isadora, Rachel. *Ben's Trumpet*. Greenwillow Books, 1979.
Ben wants to be a trumpeter, but plays only an imaginary instrument until one of the musicians in a neighborhood nightclub discovers his ambition.

Isadora, Rachel. *Lili at Ballet*. G.P. Putnam's Sons, 1993.
Lili dreams of becoming a ballerina and goes to her ballet lessons four afternoons a week.

Klagsbrun, Francine, ed. *Free to Be . . . You and Me*. McGraw Hill, 1974. Record and book.

Kuskin, Karla. *The Philharmonic Gets Dressed*. Harper & Row, 1982. The 105 members of the Philharmonic Orchestra get ready for a performance.

Littledale, Freya. *The Farmer in the Soup*. Scholastic, 1987. A farmer who thought his wife had an easy life, traded his chores for hers and discovered that it wasn't easy at all and that she did it very well indeed.

Merriam, Eve. *Mommies at Work*. Simon & Schuster, 1989. Examines many different jobs performed by working mothers, including counting money in banks and building bridges.

Miller, Margaret. *Who Uses This?* Greenwillow Books, 1990. Brief text, in question and answer form, and accompanying photographs introduce a variety of objects, their purpose, and who uses them.

Miller, Margaret. *Whose Hat?* Greenwillow Books, 1988. Color photographs of hats that represent various occupations, including a chef's cap, a construction worker's helmet, a magician's hat and a firefighter's hat.

Miller, Margaret. *Whose Shoe?* Greenwillow Books, 1991. Illustrates a variety of footwear and matches each wearer with the appropriate shoe.

Quinlan, Patricia. *My Dad Takes Care of Me*. Annick Press, 1987. A boy's father is unemployed.

Rockwell, Anne. *My Barber*. Macmillan, 1981. A young boy and his father visit their barbers.

Rockwell, Anne. ***When We Grow Up***. Dutton, 1981.
Pictures of children demonstrating the various jobs they want to have when they grow up.

Rockwell, Harlow. ***My Dentist***. Greenwillow Books, 1975.
Simple text and illustrations describe a visit to the dentist.

Rockwell, Harlow. ***My Doctor***. Macmillan, 1973.
Describes a young child's visit to the doctor's office.

Rogers, Fred. ***Going to the Doctor***. G.P. Putnam's Sons, 1986.
Describes what a child can expect to see and do on a visit to the doctor's office.

Rylant, Cynthia. ***Mr. Grigg's Work***. Orchard Books, 1989.
Mr. Griggs so loves his work at the post office that he thinks of it all the time and everything reminds him of it.

First Year

MY FAMILY TRADITIONS

Objectives

- Children will learn about the values, heritage, culture, and traditions of their own families and others.
- Children will learn about past times.
- Children will learn to understand and accept diversity in families.

Second Year

THE JOY OF GIVING

Objectives

- Children will think about various ways to express love and appreciation.
- Children will develop concern for those less fortunate.
- Children will consider the value of giving.

COMMENTARY

Sharing the Holidays

Thanksgiving is one time when many families gather to celebrate their blessings. Therefore, the focus for sharing is on the family—a topic of immediate interest to children.

The concept of "family" has been changing recently. Teachers should help children understand that a family is a group of people who live together and help each other. It is important that children learn about and appreciate each other's families. A recommended book by Norma Simon, *All Kinds of Families*, depicts many kinds of family structures and cultural lifestyles.

Children will learn about the values, heritage, culture, and traditions of their own families and others in **My Family Traditions**. The classroom might reflect the cultural backgrounds of the children's families and the community at large. By providing opportunities for parents or grandparents to participate in the classroom and help with their child's sharing contribution, the teacher conveys a sense of worth to every child. Here are some books worth noting. *The Keeping Quilt* by Patricia Polacco is about a Jewish immigrant family and the homemade quilt that ties together the lives of four generations—a symbol of their love and faith.

The Patchwork Quilt by Valerie Flourney is about a black girl who helps her grandmother and mother make a beautiful quilt that tells the story of her family's life.

Knots on a Counting Rope by Bill Martin, Jr. and John Archambault is about an Indian boy and his grandfather who reminisce about the young boy's birth, his first horse, and an exciting horse race.

The commercial aspects of Christmas are significantly played down in this curriculum. There are no books or songs about Santa Claus. Children are often excessively stimulated at this time of year and it is important to approach the holidays as an opportunity for promoting values such as generosity, concern for those less fortunate, and open-mindedness with respect to differences.

The curriculum includes Kwanzaa and Hanukkah. It is suggested that Hanukkah be introduced in November with the theme **My Family Traditions**. The book *Grandma's Latkes* by Malka Drucker is a loving story about passing down a tradition from one generation to another. The granddaughter also learns why latkes are eaten on Hanukkah and about the miracles that happened.

My Family Traditions

Letter to Parents

Dear Family:

Thanksgiving is a time when many families celebrate their values, heritage, culture, and traditions. To hear of past times through stories, songs, and memories is a valuable experience for children. This month, our theme is **My Family Traditions**. *We would like your child to share something of your family's past. Here are some ways this might be done.*

- *Bring an old toy, quilt, or object that belonged to a parent or grandparent.*

- *Share a song, game, story, or fingerplay that a grandparent remembers from childhood.*

- *Bring a grandparent to school for a visit.*

- *Tell how the child's ancestors came to this country.*

- *Share a food sample from an old family recipe.*

- *Share an old-fashioned utilitarian object or heirloom.*

- *Invite someone to demonstrate an old craft, such as spinning, weaving, candle making, rug braiding, or making crafts from corn husks.*

- *Tell about a harvest festival from the child's own background, such as Kwanzaa, or tell how the family will observe Thanksgiving Day.*

Sincerely,

Your Child's Teachers

67

THE JOY OF GIVING
LETTER TO PARENTS

Dear Family:

At this time of year, our theme is **The Joy of Giving**. Children will think about various ways in which to express love and appreciation. We will read both holiday and non-holiday books that promote the value of generosity and show the joy it brings both giver and receiver.

For sharing this month, your child may show a present he or she has made for someone else. Your child may describe how it was made, who it is for, and why that person is special.

We will also encourage children to show concern for those less fortunate. Throughout the month, children may bring in used toys in good condition to give to a hospital or shelter. They will put them under the class "Giving Tree," which is a sturdy branch set in plaster and decorated with tiny, bright red apples. We may also have small decorations in the colors of Hanukkah (blue and white) or Kwanzaa (red, black, and green).

Sincerely,

Your Child's Teachers

68

SUGGESTED ACTIVITIES FOR NOVEMBER/DECEMBER

COOKING PROJECTS

Cornbread

2 cups cornmeal
1/2 cup whole wheat pastry flour
1 tsp. salt
1/2 tsp. baking soda

2 Tbsp. honey
1 egg, beaten
2 Tbsp. oil
2 cups buttermilk

Preheat oven to 425°. Combine wet and dry ingredients separately. Stir wet and dry ingredients together. Pour into an oiled 8" x 8" (20 cm x 20 cm) pan. Bake about 20 minutes.

Apple Turkeys

Each child will need a red apple for this project. You will also need a bag of small marshmallows, a bag of large marshmallows, a bag of cranberries, a large box of raisins, a package of red licorice, and a box of non-colored toothpicks. The apples will represent the turkeys' bodies. Show children how to alternate cranberries and small marshmallows on five toothpicks and stick them into the apples for tail feathers. Help children attach large marshmallows for heads. Raisin eyes and red licorice wattles may be added as well. Apple turkeys look wonderful on a holiday party table.

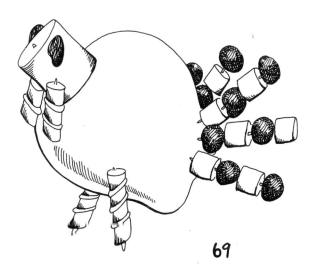

69

Experimenting With Popcorn

Read Tomie dePaola's *The Popcorn Book* to find out the history of popcorn and other interesting facts. Place a popcorn maker (without its dome lid) in the center of a group of children and watch the corn pop. Be sure children are seated well back from the popper. Invite children to make predictions about how far the popcorn will pop out of the popper. Try to obtain a variety of whole ears of popcorn for children to compare.

Christmas Tree Centerpiece

Have children bring in a plastic zipper sandwich bag filled with 1" (2.5 cm) pieces of a raw vegetable, such as carrots, celery, cherry tomatoes, broccoli, cauliflower, sweet peppers, and olives. Children might help scrub the vegetables with a brush at home. Children will use toothpicks to stick their vegetables onto a Styrofoam cone and help make a spinach-yogurt dip for the vegetables. Serve at your holiday party.

Spinach-Yogurt Dip

1 large clove garlic, peeled and minced
1 Tbsp. olive oil
1 10-oz. pkg. frozen chopped spinach, thawed and squeezed

1/2 cup plain yogurt
1/3 cup grated Parmesan
1/4 tsp. salt
1/4 tsp. pepper

Sauté garlic in oil until soft. Combine garlic and oil with remaining ingredients in a blender or food processor. Process until smooth. Cover and chill until serving.

ARTS & CRAFTS PROJECTS

I Am Thankful Montage
Cut 9" x 12" yellow construction paper on a diagonal to represent a cornucopia. Invite children to mount the cornucopias on 12" x 18" (30 cm x 45 cm) sheets of construction paper. Have them cut colorful shapes from colored paper scraps to represent harvest fruits and vegetables and glue the shapes to the cornucopia. You may wish to write or have children write, "I Am Thankful" under the cornucopias.

Macaroni and Paper Necklaces
Invite children to string alternating macaroni and colored paper squares with center holes. To help children pass the yarn through the holes, dip the ends in paraffin or diluted white glue and let dry.

Turkey Paintings
Use brown wrapping paper or an opened grocery bag. Look at pictures of turkeys—discuss how they look, how they sound, how they move. Invite children to draw turkeys on the brown paper using crayons or markers. Children may use long strips of colored paper for feathers or to cut into small pieces for decorating the body. Encourage them to add barnyard scenes as well.

HOLIDAY GIFT IDEAS

Calendar
Ask an advertising or printing company if they might donate some 3" x 3" (7.5 cm x 7.5 cm) calendars for children to use in making their own gift calendars. Children will print pictures to decorate the calendars using Styrofoam meat trays. Cut off the sides of the meat trays and print children's names on the backs. Show children how to draw pictures on the Styrofoam with a dull pencil. Squeeze a small amount of water-soluble printing ink on a piece of smooth masonite. Roll a brayer over the ink until the ink is spread as wide as the brayer. Help children roll the brayer first in the ink and then across the incised designs on the Styrofoam. The inked designs are then pressed onto pieces of light-colored construction paper and removed. When prints have dried, glue them at the top of sheets of 9" x 12" (22.5 x 30 cm) colored construction paper. Place the calendars under the prints. Punch two holes at the top and add ribbon loops for hanging.

Gift Wrap
Show children how to make their own stamps by cutting interesting shapes from strips of adhesive-backed foam mounting tape and pressing the shapes onto small wooden blocks. Children may use colored ink pads to ink their stamps. Colors may overlap. Invite children to decorate opened brown paper grocery bags with original stamps. They may use the gift wrap for their gift calendars.

Hanging Pine Cones
Collect and ask parents to collect pine cones in a variety of sizes. Attach a yarn or string loop to each pine cone. Show children how to hold pine cones by the strings and drag them through a tray of white tempera paint mixed with a little white glue. Help them cover all sides of the pine cones. Invite children to sprinkle gold, silver, or clear glitter on the pine cones while they are still tacky. Pine cones should dry on a sheet of waxed paper. Use as tree ornaments or to hang on doorknobs.

Sachets
Using pinking shears, cut a 5" x 5" (12.5 cm x 12.5 cm) piece of calico fabric for each child. Provide sweetly scented items, such as whole cloves, cedar chips, broken pieces of cinnamon bark, bits of orange peel, or pine needles, for children to place in the center. Children may gather up the corners and hold them while the teacher tightly wraps the bundles with small rubber bands. Add bows of thin silk ribbon. You may wish to provide calico squares and ribbons of various colors. The sachets will look attractive in a basket in the classroom before children take them home.

Cinnamon Hearts
1 1/2 cups ground cinnamon
1 cup applesauce

Mix cinnamon and applesauce together. Help children roll out the mixture between sheets of waxed paper to 1/4" (6.25 mm) thickness. Cut out hearts using a heart-shaped cookie cutter. Before the ornaments dry, make small holes through which to thread thin silk ribbons. Ornaments will dry overnight on waxed paper. These make attractive tree ornaments or room fresheners.

Brick Bookends
Show children how to make montages on the bricks using colored magazine pictures and white glue. Spray the completed bookends with high-gloss varnish or wrap with clear self-adhesive plastic. These work as doorstops too—glue on felt rectangles cut to fit the bottoms (largest rectangle) of the bricks.

72

ADDITIONAL IDEAS AND PROJECTS

Hungry Turkeys
Glue an Ellison-die turkey shape to a piece of cardstock for each child. Draw a circle on each paper to represent the turkey's food dish and write a number on the dish. Invite children to glue the appropriate number of popcorn kernels on the turkey's dish. Pilgrim shapes may be substituted for the turkeys.

Place Settings
Give each child a piece of cardstock to use as a placemat. Have children glue small paper plates in the center of the placemats. Provide Ellison-die forks, knives, and spoons for children to glue in place. Encourage children to decorate their placemats and draw Thanksgiving dinner on their plates. You may wish to provide holiday paper napkins for children to glue on as well.

Stocking Secrets
Place some seasonal items, such as a dreidel, a small menorah, or a candy cane, inside a Christmas stocking. Invite children to feel the stocking and guess the shapes inside.

Memory
Place several seasonal items, such as stocking toys, nuts, candy canes, dreidels, or Kwanzaa items, in a stocking. Remove them one at a time and discuss them with children. Replace all the items in the stocking. Then reintroduce all but one. Challenge children to tell you which item is still inside the stocking.

Classroom Experience Charts
Pose questions such as the following to children. Create experience charts using their replies. Help children recognize their likenesses and differences.

What are you thankful for?
What do you like to eat at Thanksgiving?
Who comes to your house for the holidays?
How do you help your family prepare for Thanksgiving?

Over the River Traditional Song by Lydia Maria Child

1. O - ver the ri - ver and thru the wood to Grand - fa - ther's house we go.   The
2. O - ver the ri - ver and thru the wood trot fast   my dap - ple gray.   Spring

horse knows the way to   car - ry   the sleigh thru the white and drift - ed   snow,
o - ver the ground like   a hunt - ing hound for this   is Thanks - giv - ing   day.

O - ver the ri - ver and   thru the wood, Oh how the wind does   blow.   It
O - ver the   ri - ver and   thru the wood, now Grand - mo - ther's face I spy.   Hur -

stings the nose and bites the toes as   o - ver the ground we   go.
rah for the fun! Is the pud - ding done? Hur - rah for the pump - kin   pie!

RELATED SONGS

Elf Helpers

Traditional

Tap, tap, tap, tap, go our lit-tle ham-mers.

Ring, ring, ring, ring, go our lit-tle bells.

We are lit-tle help-ers, tap-a-tap-a-tap tap.

We are lit-tle help-ers bring-ng some-one joy.

Children may use rhythm sticks and bells.

FEATURED BOOK

Galdone, Paul. *The Elves and the Shoemaker*. Clarion Books, 1984.

When the poor shoemaker and his wife discover the two little elves who have helped them have no clothes, they sew fine outfits for them.

Christmas Is Coming

Old English Carol

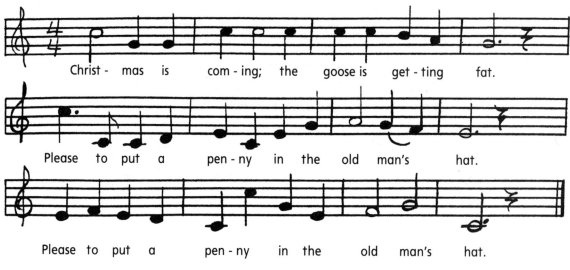

Christ - mas is com - ing; the goose is get - ting fat.

Please to put a pen - ny in the old man's hat.

Please to put a pen - ny in the old man's hat.

FEATURED BOOK

Gackenbach, Dick. ***Claude the Dog: A Christmas Story***. Seabury Press, 1974.

Claude the dog gives away all his Christmas presents to a down-and-out friend but receives an even better present from his young owner.

Holiday Books

African-American Christmas and Kwanzaa

Bryan, Ashley. *I'm Going to Sing: Black American Spirituals.* Vol II. Atheneum, 1982.

Chocolate, Deborah. *Kwanzaa.* Childrens Press, 1990.
>Discusses the holiday in which African Americans celebrate their roots and cultural heritage from Africa.

Langstaff, John. *What a Morning! The Christmas Story in Black Spirituals.* Margaret K. McElderry Books, 1987.
>Five illustrated spirituals dealing with the birth of Christ on the first Christmas morning.

Pinkney, Andrea Davis. *Seven Candles for Kwanzaa.* Dial Books, 1993.
>Describes the origins and practices of Kwanzaa, a seven-day holiday in which African Americans celebrate their ancestral values.

Shoemaker, Kathryn. *Children, Go Where I Send Thee: An American Spiritual.* Winston Press, 1980.
>The text of an American spiritual, originally sung by slave congregations on Christmas eve.

Hanukkah

Drucker, Malka. *Grandma's Latkes.* Harcourt Brace Jovanovich, 1992.
>Grandma explains the meaning of Hanukkah while showing Molly how to cook latkes for the holiday.

Hirsh, Marilyn. *I Love Hanukkah.* Holiday House, 1984.
>A young boy describes his family's celebration of Hanukkah and all the things he likes about the holiday.

Penn, Malka. *The Miracle of the Potato Latkes.* Holiday House, 1994.
>Tante Golda makes the best latkes in all of Russia to share with her friends at Hanukkah. Even when a poor harvest leaves her with no potatoes, she is certain that "God will provide."

Schotter, Roni. *Hanukkah!* Joy Street Books, 1990.
>Describes the meaning and traditions of Hanukkah as five children and their family celebrate the holiday.

Discovering the Holidays Through Our Five Senses

Allington, Richard. *Beginning to Learn about Smelling*. Raintree Children's Books, 1980.
> Describes the fourteen categories of aromas, including those associated with holidays, cleanliness, and illness.

Allington, Richard. *Beginning to Learn about Tasting*. Raintree Children's Books, 1980.
> Introduces the four basic tastes—sweet, sour, bitter and salty—along with fifteen other types of tastes and textures, such as spicy, cold, and crunchy. Recipes and activities are included.

Allington, Richard. *Beginning to Learn about Touching*. Raintree Children's Books, 1980.
> Explores the touch and feel of objects that are scratchy, warm, squishy, bumpy, and so on. Includes activities.

Cook, Scott. *The Gingerbread Boy*. Alfred A. Knopf, 1987.
> A gingerbread boy runs away from the woman who made him and from several other creatures who wish to eat him, but a clever fox proves his undoing.

Galdone, Paul. *The Gingerbread Boy*. Seabury Press, 1975.
> The gingerbread boy eludes the hungry grasp of everyone he meets until he happens upon a fox more clever than he.

Kimmel, Eric. *The Chanukkah Guest*. Holiday House, 1990.
> On the first night of Chanukkah, Old Bear wanders into Bubba Brayna's house and receives a delicious helping of potato latkes when she mistakes him for the rabbi.

Kimmel, Eric. *The Gingerbread Man*. Holiday House, 1993.
> A freshly baked gingerbread man escapes when he is taken out of the oven and eludes a number of clever animals until he meets a clever fox.

Polacco, Patricia. *Uncle Vova's Tree*. Philomel Books, 1989.
> Grandparents, aunts and uncles, and children gather at a farmhouse to celebrate Christmas in the Russian tradition.

MY FAMILY TRADITIONS

RELATED PICTURE BOOKS

Aliki. ***The Two of Them***. Greenwillow Books, 1979.
Describes the relationship of a grandfather and his
granddaughter from her birth to his death.

Anderson, Joan. ***The First Thanksgiving Feast***. Clarion Books, 1984.
Recreates the first harvest feast celebrated by Pilgrims in
1621. Uses Pilgrim and Indian actors and the seventeenth-
century setting of Plimoth Plantation, a living history museum
in Plymouth, Massachusetts, to reenact Thanksgiving.

Beil, Karen. ***Grandma According to Me***. Doubleday, 1992.
A young girl shows how much she loves her grandmother
by telling her what she likes about her.

Blegvad, Lenore. ***Once Upon a Time and Grandma***. Margaret K.
McElderry Books, 1993.
When her grandchildren come for a visit, Grandma shows
them the apartment where she lived and talks about what
she did when she was a young girl.

Bornstein, Ruth. ***A Beautiful Seashell***. Harper & Row, 1990.
Rosie and great-grandmother spend a quiet time together
as great-grandmother tells a story from her childhood in
the old country.

Brooks, Ron. ***Timothy and Gramps***. Bradbury Press, 1978.
Timothy enjoys school more after his grandfather's visit to
his classroom.

Buckley, Helen and Jan Ormerod. ***Grandmother and I***. Lothrop,
Lee & Shepard, 1994.
A child considers how Grandmother's lap is just right for
those times when lightning is coming in the window or the
cat is missing.

Buckley, Helen and Jan Ormerod. ***Grandfather and I***. Lothrop,
Lee & Shepard, 1994.
Grandfather is the perfect person to spend time with
because he is never in a hurry.

Burningham, John. ***Grandpa***. Crown Publishing, 1985.
A little girl and her grandfather share very special moments.

Carlstrom, Nancy. ***The Moon Came Too***. Macmillan, 1987.
A young child excitedly plans all the essentials he must take with him on a trip to Grandma's house.

Caseley, Judith. ***When Grandpa Came to Stay***. Greenwillow Books, 1986.
When Grandpa comes to his house to stay, Benny enjoys his company and helps him cope with Grandma's death.

Child, Lydia. ***Over the River and Through the Wood***. Coward, McCann & Gevghegan, 1974.
Verses to the traditional Thanksgiving story are illustrated from both Grandmother's and the journeying family's point of view.

Drescher, Joan. ***Your Family, My Family***. Walker, 1980.
Briefly describes several kinds of families and cites some of the strengths of family life.

Drucker, Malka. ***Grandma's Latkes***. Harcourt Brace Jovanovich, 1992.
Grandma explains the meaning of Hanukkah while showing Molly how to cook latkes for the holiday.

Falwell, Cathryn. ***Feast for 10***. Clarion Books, 1993.
Numbers from one to ten are used to tell how members of a family shop and work together to prepare a meal.

Flourney, Valerie. ***The Patchwork Quilt***. Dial Books, 1985.
Using scraps cut from the family's old clothing, Tanya helps her grandmother and mother make a beautiful quilt that tells the story of her family's life.

Hall, Donald. ***Ox-Cart Man***. Viking Press, 1979.
Describes the day-to-day life throughout the changing seasons of an early 19th-century New England family.

Highwater, Jamake. ***Moonsong Lullaby***. Lothrop, Lee & Shepard, 1981.
As the moon moves across the sky, it observes the activities of an Indian camp and of the natural phenomena surrounding it.

Johnson, Angela. ***Tell Me A Story, Mama***. Orchard Books, 1989.
A young African-American girl and her mother remember together all the girl's favorite stories about her mother's childhood.

Johnston, Tony. ***The Quilt Story***. G. P. Putnam's Sons, 1985.
A pioneer mother lovingly stitches a beautiful quilt which warms and comforts her daughter Abigail; many years later another mother mends and patches it for her little girl.

Johnston, Tony. ***Yonder***. Dial Books, 1987.
As the plum tree changes in the passing seasons, so do the lives of a three-generation farm family.

Jonas, Ann. ***The Quilt***. Greenwillow Books, 1984.
A child's new patchwork quilt recalls adventures at bedtime.

Lester, Alison. ***Isabella's Bed***. Houghton Mifflin, 1993.
Anna and Luis' grandmother at last shares her important personal history of her younger days in South America.

Levinson, Riki. ***Watch the Stars Come Out***. Dutton, 1985.
Grandma tells about her mama's journey to America by boat years ago.

Lindbergh, Reeve. ***Grandfather's Lovesong***. Viking, 1993.
A poetic description of love between a boy and his grandfather, using metaphors of nature throughout the season.

Locker, Thomas. ***Where the River Begins***. Dial Books, 1984.
Two young boys and their grandfather go on a camping trip to find the source of the river that flows by their home.

Lyon, George. ***Who Came Down That Road?*** Orchard Books, 1992.
Mother and child ponder the past in discussing who might have traveled down an old, old road, looking backwards from pioneer settlers all the way to prehistoric animals.

Martin, Bill, Jr. and John Archambault. ***Knots on a Counting Rope***. Henry Holt, 1987.
Boy-Strength-of-Blue-Horses and his grandfather reminisce about the young boy's birth, his first horse, and an exciting horse race.

McFarlane, Sheryl. ***Waiting for the Whales***. Philomel Books, 1991.
A lonely old man who waits each year to see the orcas swim past his house imparts his love of whales to his granddaughter.

Miles, Miska. ***Annie and the Old One***. Little, Brown, 1971.
Annie, a young Navaho girl, can't imagine life without her grandmother—the old one. She refuses to believe that when the new rug is taken from the loom, her grandmother will die. This story tells how Annie plots to slow down the weaving in order to hold back time.

Polacco, Patricia. ***The Keeping Quilt***. Simon & Schuster, 1988.
A homemade quilt ties together the lives of four generations of an immigrant Jewish family, remaining a symbol of their enduring love and faith.

Rand, Gloria. ***The Cabin Key***. Harcourt Brace Jovanovich, 1994.
Reveling in the atmosphere of her family's mountain cabin, a young girl remembers the many stories she has heard about previous generations and their adventures with the area's wildlife.

Raynor, Dorka. ***Grandparents Around the World***. Albert Whitman, 1980.
Presents forty-six full-page photographs of grandparents and children taken in twenty-five countries with a brief identifying text accompanying each photo.

Rockwell, Anne and Harlow. ***When I Go Visiting***. Macmillan, 1984.
A child describes a thoroughly enjoyable visit with Grandmother and Grandfather in their city apartment.

Rylant, Cynthia. ***When I Was Young in the Mountains***. Dutton, 1982.
Reminiscences of the pleasures of life in the mountains as a child.

Shelby, Anne. ***Homeplace***. Orchard Books, 1995.
A grandmother and grandchild trace their family history.

Simon, Norma. ***All Kinds of Families***. Albert Whitman, 1976.
Explores in words and pictures what a family is and how families vary in makeup and lifestyle.

THE JOY OF GIVING
RELATED PICTURE BOOKS (CHRISTMAS)

Brown, Margaret Wise. ***The Little Fir Tree***. Harper & Row, 1954.
At the edge of the forest, the little lame boy's father finds the perfect tree for his son to grow strong with.

Bunting, Eve. ***Night Tree***. Harcourt Brace Jovanovich, 1991.
A family makes its annual pilgrimage to decorate an evergreen tree with food for the forest animals at Christmas time.

Cole, Joanna. ***A Gift from Saint Francis: The First Crèche***. Morrow, 1989.
Traces the life of the Italian who turned his back on his family's wealth to help the poor. Discusses Francis' role in the making of the first crèche.

DePaola, Tomie. ***The Friendly Beasts: An Old English Christmas Carol***. G.P. Putnam's Sons, 1981.
In this old English Christmas carol, the friendly beasts tell of the gifts they have given to the newborn Jesus.

Delton, Judy. ***The Perfect Christmas Gift***. Macmillan, 1992.
Bear is distressed by his inability to find the perfect Christmas present for Duck until Rabbit points out that the true significance of the holiday is having friends.

Gackenbach, Dick. ***Claude the Dog: A Christmas Story***. Seabury Press, 1974.
Claude the dog gives away all his Christmas presents to a down-and-out friend but receives an even better present from his young owner.

Johnston, Tony. ***Pages of Music***. G.P. Putnam's Sons, 1988.
A childhood visit to Sardinia haunts a composer, who returns there one Christmas to repay with his music the kindness of the island's inhabitants.

Kimura, Yuriko. *Christmas Present from a Friend*. Abingdon Press, 1985.
> A rabbit shares the joy of Christmas with his friends and finds that it is returned several times over.

Moeri, Louise. *Star Mother's Youngest Child*. Houghton Mifflin, 1975.
> The grumpy old woman had never properly celebrated Christmas until the year that the Star Mother's youngest child came to earth to find out what Christmas was all about.

Scheidl, Gerda. *Miriam's Gift*. North-South Books, 1989.
> Elias, a shepherd, takes leave of his daughter Miriam in order to welcome baby Jesus. Elias says that Miriam must stay behind but her faith allows her to overcome obstacles and give baby Jesus her own special gift.

RELATED PICTURE BOOKS (HANUKKAH)

Goldin, Barbara Diamond. *Just Enough Is Plenty*. Viking Kestrel, 1988.
> With Hanukkah about to begin, Malka is worried because her family is so poor, but when a poor stranger comes to the door, her generous family cannot turn him away.

Jaffe, Nina. *In the Month of Kislev*. Viking, 1992.
> A rich, arrogant merchant takes the family of a poor peddler to court and learns a lesson about the meaning of Hanukkah.

Manushkin, Fran. *Latkes and Applesauce*. Scholastic, 1990.
> When a blizzard leaves a family house-bound one Hanukkah, they share what little they have with some starving animals who later return the favor.

THE JOY OF GIVING

RELATED PICTURE BOOKS (NON-HOLIDAY)

Bang, Molly. **The Paper Crane**. Greenwillow Books, 1985.
  A mysterious man enters a restaurant and pays for his dinner
  with a paper crane that magically comes alive and dances.

Flack, Marjorie. **Ask Mr. Bear**. Macmillan, 1971.
  A little boy hunts for a present to give to his mother for her
  birthday.

Galdone, Paul. **The Elves and the Shoemaker**. Clarion Books, 1984.
  When the poor shoemaker and his wife discover the two
  naked little elves who have helped them become successful,
  they sew fine outfits for them.

Gray, Nigel. **Little Pig's Tale**. Macmillan, 1990.
  Almost all of Little Pig's attempts at finding the right present
  for his mother's birthday fail, but his last idea is just right.

Grimm Brothers. **The Falling Stars**. North-South Books, 1985.
  A poor child who possesses nothing but the clothes on her
  back gives everything away to others who are suffering and
  receives a reward from the heavens.

Hughes, Shirley. **Giving**. Candlewick Press, 1993.
  A little girl and her baby brother experience the various
  aspects of giving, finding that it is nice whether you are giving
  a present, a smile, or a kiss.

Humphrey, Margo. **The River that Gave Gifts: An Afro-American Story**.
Children's Book Press, 1987.
  Four children each make their own special gift to the beloved
  elderly women of the town.

Kiser, SuAnn. **The Birthday Thing**. Greenwillow Books, 1989.
  Timothy's family "helps" him create a birthday thing that turns
  out to be exactly what his mother needed for her birthday.

Littledale, Freya. ***The Elves and the Shoemaker***. Four Winds Press, 1975.
A Grimm's fairy tale about the poor old shoemaker who becomes successful with the help of two elves who finish his shoes during the night.

Pearson, Susan. ***Happy Birthday, Grampie***. Dial Books, 1987.
Martha gives her blind grandfather, now living in a home for the aged, a birthday gift to remember.

Polacco, Patricia. ***Chicken Sunday***. Philomel Books, 1992.
To thank old Eula for her wonderful Sunday chicken dinners, the children sell decorated eggs and buy her a beautiful Easter hat.

Rodanas, Kristina. ***The Story of Wali Dâd***. Lothrop, Lee & Shepard, 1988.
The desire of a poor, old grass cutter in India to share what little he has with a kind and beautiful woman begins an incredible chain of events.

Sawicki, Norma. ***Something for Mom***. Lothrop, Lee & Shepard, 1987.
Matilda struggles to give her mother a birthday surprise.

Shannon, George. ***The Surprise***. Greenwillow Books, 1983.
Squirrel gives his mother a special surprise on her birthday.

Silverstein, Shel. ***The Giving Tree***. Harper & Row, 1964.
This is the story of a tree who loved a little boy so much that she gave him everything—her apples, her branches, and finally her trunk.

Sis, Peter. ***Going Up! A Color Counting Book***. Greenwillow Books, 1989.
As the elevator moves up from the first floor to the twelfth, various people dressed in different colors get on, all bound for a birthday surprise.

Watts, Bernadette. ***The Elves and the Shoemaker***. North-South, 1986.
The poor old shoemaker becomes successful with the help of two elves who finish his shoes during the night.

Weiss, Nicki. ***Surprise Box***. G. P. Putnam's Sons, 1991.
A girl explores her surroundings both outdoors and indoors, examining clover, ant, dandelion, and a surprise present.

JANUARY

First Year

TOYS ON PARADE

Objectives

• Children will share their toys.

• Children will learn to respect the possessions of others.

Second Year

RING OUT THE OLD, RING IN THE NEW!

Objectives

• Children will build language skills as they learn about opposites.

• Children will gain exposure to the idea of enduring value as opposed to fad.

COMMENTARY

January Topics

After the holidays, children will have the opportunity to share some toys.

During **Toys on Parade**, special days are designated for these traditional toys: wind-up toys, teddy bears, balls, jack-in-the-boxes or toys with springs, dolls, toys with wheels, and tops or spinning toys. These days include special movement, game, or song activities. For example, the teacher may plan a movement game in which children are "wind-up toys" that move to music. As the music slows down and becomes quieter, children respond accordingly. When the music finally stops, children "freeze."

Ring Out the Old, Ring In the New! suggests the new year while providing opportunities for continued sharing of old and new toys. James Stevenson's book, *The Night After Christmas*, tells of a teddy bear and doll that are thrown away after Christmas when they are replaced by newer toys. Fortunately, they are befriended by a stray dog and find a new home. This book affords an opportunity to talk about recycling toys or items children do not wish to keep.

This theme also leads to an exploration of the concept of opposites. Activities are planned to build language development. For example, children might make shiny and then dull paintings, rough and then smooth paintings, high and then low constructions, soft and hard collages, and so forth. Many traditional children's songs, such as "Jack Be Nimble," "Deedle, Deedle, Dumpling" and "Pease Porridge Hot," reinforce ideas as high and low, off and on, hot and cold.

References

Goodman, K. *What's the Whole in Whole Language?* Heinemann, 1986.

Graves, D. *Build a Literate Classroom.* Heinemann, 1991.

TOYS ON PARADE
LETTER TO PARENTS

Dear Family:

Our procedure for sharing time will be somewhat different this month. Children may share as many times as desired, so long as the shared item fits the theme for the particular day. For our theme **Toys on Parade**, we are emphasizing traditional rather than fad toys. Please label all toys with your child's name. It is important to tell us whether or not the toy may be shared with other children.

The calendar will indicate which day to bring the following toys:

- wind-up toys
- teddy bears
- balls
- dolls
- jack-in-the-boxes (or toys with springs)
- toys with wheels
- tops (or spinning toys)

Sincerely,

Your Child's Teachers

89

Ring Out the Old, Ring In the New!

Letter to Parents

Dear Family:

Happy New Year! This month, we will **Ring Out the Old, Ring In the New!**

For sharing time this month, we ask that your child bring in two similar toys or objects. One should be old, the other new. Your child will enjoy talking about them and making contrasts. Sometimes it is the old toy or object that is the more beloved. The children's sharing will lead us to explore the concept of opposites, thereby building language skills.

Sincerely,

Your Child's Teachers

SUGGESTED ACTIVITIES FOR JANUARY

COOKING PROJECT

Baking Powder Biscuits

1/2 cup shortening
2 cups flour
1 Tbsp. sugar

1 Tbsp. baking powder
1 tsp. salt
3/4 cup milk

Preheat oven to 450°. Cut shortening into flour, sugar, baking powder, and salt with pastry blender until mixture resembles fine crumbs. Stir in milk until dough leaves side of bowl. Dough will be soft and sticky. Turn dough onto lightly-floured surface. Knead lightly. Roll or pat 1/2" (1.25 cm) thick. Cut with floured round cutter. Place biscuits on ungreased cookie sheet about 1" (2.5 cm) apart for crusty sides, touching for soft sides. Bake until golden brown, 10 to 12 minutes. Immediately remove from cookie sheet. Makes 1 dozen biscuits.

ART PROJECT

Village in Winter

Collect small milk cartons from a school cafeteria to make into little houses for children to paint. Adding liquid dishwashing detergent to paint can help the paint stick to the waxy cartons. Show children how to glue little squares of construction paper in an overlapping pattern to make roof shingles. They may also glue yellow squares to the sides of their cartons to make windows. Invite students to make a door that opens by cutting around three sides of a rectangle. Discarded holiday cards may be used for pictures to add to the scene. Leave tabs at the bottom so pictures can stand. A large sheet of cardboard or plywood covered with cotton batting maybe used to make the ground. Add an aluminum foil skating pond. Arrange the houses to make a village. Discuss the sights and sounds of a winter scene.

TOYS ON PARADE
RELATED ARTS & CRAFTS PROJECTS

Wind-Up Toy Day
Cut out a wind-up key for each child from gray construction paper. Read *Alexander and the Wind-up Mouse* by Leo Lionni to the class. Give wind-up keys to the children as motivational starters for illustrations. Invite them to glue the keys to sheets of drawing paper and complete the toys. Or you may wish to have wind-up keys already glued onto art paper.

Jack-in-the-Box Day
Show children how to make accordion springs from strips of paper. Provide a supply of construction paper circles and rectangles. Invite children to use their paper springs as arms, legs, tails, and necks as they create paper dolls or puppets by combining the springs with circles and rectangles. Details may be added with crayons or markers.

Teddy Bear Day
After reading *Alphabears* by Kathleen Hague, invite children to draw or paint pictures of teddy bears. The bears are given the children's own names. Children may describe the personality characteristics of their bears. Add children's words to their papers as they dictate.

Doll Day

Invite children to draw pictures of themselves with pastel dye sticks on pieces of muslin. Cut around the children's drawings and stitch them to backings. Invite parent volunteers to assist you. Lightly stuff the dolls to make soft sculptures. They might be saved for a bulletin board display, such as "Dancing Around the Maypole."

Toys with Wheels Day

Show children how they might use macaroni wheels for collages or in combination with drawings of some things that have wheels. Pasta may be colored by soaking in a solution of rubbing alcohol and food coloring. The longer the pasta sits in the solution, the more intense the color. Dry pasta wheels on waxed paper before using.

Top or Spinning Toy Day

There are several commercial versions of spin painting you may wish to try with children. Alternatively, try the spinning tops that spin on ball-point pens or fine-tipped colored markers, making interesting squiggly designs as they spin. Children may add details to the spin or squiggle art as they see fit.

Ball Day

Give children each a 1" (2.5 cm) circle as a motivational starter and have them glue it onto a sheet of light-colored construction paper. Explain that the circle will become a favorite ball that they are playing with in the picture. For example, children may wish to turn the circle into a basketball, football, soccer, tennis, golf, or baseball. They may then add themselves and any other details they wish to the picture.

RING OUT THE OLD, RING IN THE NEW!

RELATED ARTS & CRAFTS PROJECTS—OPPOSITES

Black/White Collages

Invite children to glue bits of white yarn, cotton balls, buttons, white doilies, white turkey feathers, white eggshells, newsprint, popcorn, white beans, white sand, and so on to pieces of black matboard. Children may write their names with white crayon or white chalk.

Hard/Soft Collages

For soft materials, use feathers, felt, fluffy gerbil bedding, batting, cotton balls, and so on. For hard materials, use buttons, beans, corn kernels, bottle caps, macaroni shapes, and so on. Children may arrange items from both categories into collages on matboard or tagboard.

Smooth/Rough Paintings

Add sawdust to tempera to give a rough texture. Invite children to create paintings using both rough and smooth paint. You may wish to use smooth, white paint and rough, black paint to further emphasize "opposites."

Shiny/Dull Paintings

Add corn syrup to tempera to give the paint a sheen. Invite children to create paintings using both dull and shiny paint. Discuss with children which colors might be considered opposites other than black and white. Make their choices available for these projects.

Happy/Sad Mood Paintings

Do a happy painting one day. Discuss with children colors that make them happy. Play happy music in the background as they paint. On another day, talk about colors that make children sad. Play somber music and invite children to paint with sad colors.

High/Low Projects

Invite children to make flat designs on construction paper using strips of colored paper and white glue. Then show them how to use the strips of colored paper to create elevated or three-dimensional designs.

Summer/Winter Collages

Give children sheets of colored construction paper that have been divided in half either by folding or ruling. On top of one side, glue a yellow sun shape. On top of the other side, glue a white snowflake shape. Invite children to draw or cut out magazine pictures that indicate either warm weather or cold weather clothing and activities to glue on the appropriately-labeled sides of the papers.

RELATED ARTS & CRAFTS PROJECTS—NEW YEAR

New Year's Hats
Cut a slit from the edge to the center of a colored paper plate for each child. Overlap plates at the slits and staple into cone shapes. Attach elastic bands to hold hats on and invite children to paint and decorate their hats.

Noisemaking Instruments
Invite children to explore the making of rhythm instruments from common household items, such as paper bags, pots and pans, pot lids, wire brushes and screens, washboards and thimbles, kitchen spoons, coffee cans, boxes, tin shakers, tin cans, cardboard tissue tubes, combs, and rubber bands. *Listen!* by Joy Wilt and Terre Watson (Creative Resources, 1977) provides many ideas for drums, zithers, kazoos, maracas, and other instruments easily made by children.

ADDITIONAL IDEAS AND PROJECTS

Sweet/Sour Tasting
Invite children to try bits of sour pickle, sauerkraut, and sour lemonade. Then have them try sweet tastes, such as maple sugar candy, raisins, ripe banana, or chocolate. Experiment to see which part of the tongue registers sweet and which registers sour.

Contrast Games
Encourage children to recite rhymes or speak their names in a variety of voices. They may whisper, then shout. They may speak in high voices, then low ones. They may speak fast, then slow.

Classifying Objects
Label some boxes rough and smooth, shiny and dull, soft and hard, rigid and pliable, light and dark, and so on. Provide objects for sorting, such as dried beans, pebbles, felt scraps, or a mixture of items. Encourage children to sort items into the appropriate boxes.

TOYS ON PARADE
RELATED SONGS

Miss Polly Had a Dolly

Traditional

Miss Pol-ly had a dol-ly that was sick, sick, sick. She
called for the doc-tor to come quick, quick, quick.

2. The doctor came with his bag and hat
   He knocked on the door with a rat tat tat.

3. He looked at the dolly and he shook his head.
   He said, "Miss Polly, put her straight to bed."

4. He wrote on some paper for a pill, pill, pill.
   "I'll be back in the morning with the bill, bill, bill!"

Roll That Ball

Folk Tune

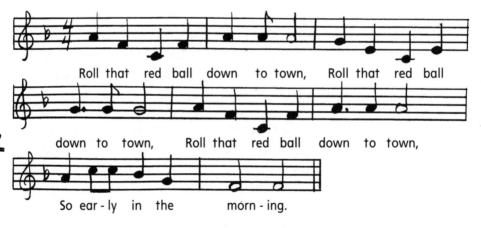

Roll that red ball down to town, Roll that red ball
down to town, Roll that red ball down to town,
So ear-ly in the morn-ing.

Bounce and catch it,
Bounce and catch it,
Bounce and catch the ball;
Bounce and catch it,
Bounce and catch it,
Do not let it fall!

I see a ball.
And I see a ball.
And a great big ball I see.
Shall we count them? Are you ready?
One! Two! Three!

TOYS ON PARADE

RELATED SONGS

Teddy Bear, Teddy Bear

Traditional

Ted - dy Bear, Ted - dy Bear, turn a - round.

Ted - dy Bear, Ted - dy Bear, touch the ground.

Ted - dy Bear, Ted - dy Bear, show your shoe.

Ted - dy Bear, Ted - dy Bear, that will do!

2. Teddy Bear, Teddy Bear, go upstairs,
   Teddy Bear, Teddy Bear, say your prayers,
   Teddy Bear, Teddy Bear, turn off the light.
   Teddy Bear, Teddy Bear, say good-night.

Pop! Goes the Weasel

Traditional

All a - round the cob - bler's bench, The mon -key chased the weas - el. The

mon - key thought 'twas all in fun. Pop! goes the weas - el.

Have children bury thumbs in fists and then pop them out. Or children may crouch on floor and then jump up.

Jack-in-the-box sits so still.
Won't you come out? Yes, I will!

TOYS ON PARADE

RELATED SONGS

The Wheels on the Bus

Traditional

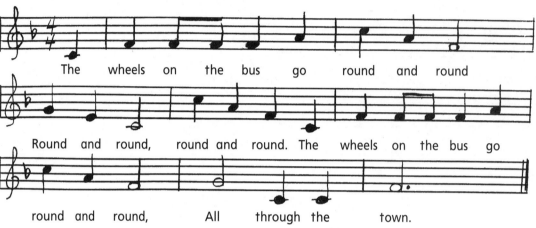

The wheels on the bus go round and round

Round and round, round and round. The wheels on the bus go

round and round, All through the town.

2. The people on the bus go up and down . . .

3. The horn on the bus goes toot, toot, toot . . .

4. The money on the bus goes clink, clink, clink . . .

5. The wipers on the bus go swish, swish, swish . . .

6. The driver on the bus says, "Move on back . . ."

Bracken, Carolyn. **The Busy School Bus**. Grosset and Dunlap, 1986.

Board book shaped like a school bus with real moving wheels.

RING OUT THE OLD, RING IN THE NEW!
RELATED SONGS

New Year Bells

Traditional English Tune

Ding, dong, ding, dong; Ding, dong, ding, dong; Ding, dong, ding, dong;

Ding, dong, ding, dong. Ring out the old; ring in the new.

Ring out the false; ring in the true.

Game

Invite children to stand in a circle with arms around each other's shoulders, swaying from side to side as they sing. At the end of the song, everyone "chimes" 1-2-3-4-5-6-7-8-9-10-11-12. After "12," everyone may jump up and shout, "Happy New Year!" Encourage children to play their noisemakers as well.

I saw three ships come sailing by,
Come sailing by, come sailing by,
I saw three ships come sailing by,
On New Year's Day in the morning.

And what do you think was in them then,
Was in them then, was in them then?
And what do you think was in them then?
On New Year's Day in the morning?

Three pretty girls were in them then,
Were in them then, were in them then,
Three pretty girls were in them then,
On New Year's Day in the morning.

One could whistle, and one could sing,
And one could play the violin;
Such joy there was at my wedding,
On New Year's Day in the morning.

— Mother Goose

The Grand Old Duke of York

The grand old Duke of York, He had ten thou-sand men. He marched them up to the top of the hill and marched them down a-gain.

2. And when they're up, they're up,
   And when they're down, they're down.
   And when they're only half-way up
   They're neither up nor down.

This song involves the use of opposites *up* and *down*. Invite children to march in place with hands in salute. When they sing *up*, children stand up tall. When *down* is sung, children crouch down. At *half-way up*, children bend in the middle.

FEATURED BOOK

John Burningham's Opposites. Crown Publishers, 1991.

Introduces the concept of opposites through labeled pictures of a boy interacting with a thin pig and a fat pig, a hot dragon and a cold snowman, and other creatures and situations.

RING OUT THE OLD, RING IN THE NEW!
RELATED SONGS

Looby Loo

Old English Singing Game

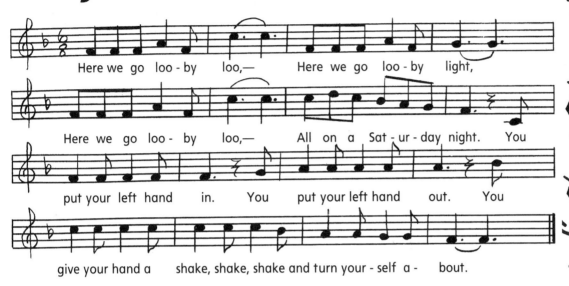

Here we go loo-by loo,— Here we go loo-by light,

Here we go loo-by loo,— All on a Sat-ur-day night. You

put your left hand in. You put your left hand out. You

give your hand a shake, shake, shake and turn your-self a-bout.

This song involves the use of opposites *left/right* and *in/out*. The song may be repeated using right hand, left leg, right leg, and so on. Here is another verse to add to illustrate up/down and backward/forward.

Here we go up, up, up.
Here we go down, down, down.
Here we go backward and forward,
Here we go 'round and around.

FEATURED BOOK

McMillan, Bruce. **Becca Backward, Becca Frontward: A Book of Opposites**. Lothrop, Lee & Shepard, 1986.

Photographs of a girl involved in various activities illustrate such opposite concepts as above/below, full/empty, and big/small.

RING OUT THE OLD, RING IN THE NEW!
RELATED SONGS

Jack Be Nimble

Mother Goose

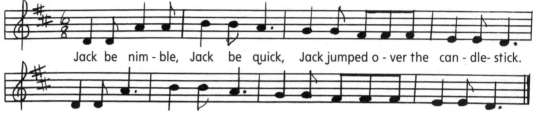

Jack be nim - ble, Jack be quick, Jack jumped o - ver the can - dle- stick.

Jack jumped high, Jack jumped low; Jack jumped o - ver and burned his toe.

This song involves the use of opposites *high* and *low*. You may wish to substitute the name of a child who may jump over a "candlestick."

Deedle, Deedle Dumpling

Mother Goose

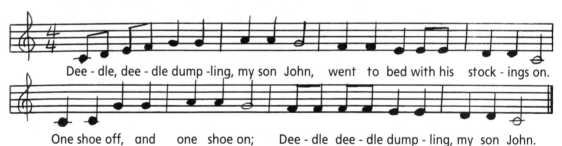

Dee - dle, dee - dle dump -ling, my son John, went to bed with his stock - ings on.

One shoe off, and one shoe on; Dee - dle dee - dle dump - ling, my son John.

This song involves the opposites *on* and *off*.

FEATURED BOOK

Hoban, Tana. *Exactly the Opposite*. Greenwillow Books, 1990.

Photographs of familiar outdoor scenes illustrate pairs of opposites.

Pease Porridge Hot

Traditional

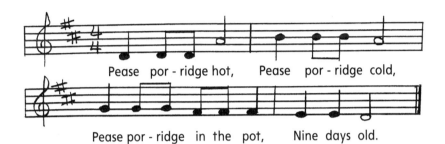

Pease por-ridge hot, Pease por-ridge cold,

Pease por-ridge in the pot, Nine days old.

This song involves the opposites *hot* and *cold*.

Partner Game (traditional)

Pease—*slap knees*
Porridge—*clap own hands*
hot—*clap partner's hands*
(Repeat on "pease porridge cold")
Pease—*slap knees*
porridge—*clap own hands*
in the—*clap right hand with partner*
pot—*clap own hands*
nine—*clap left hand with partner*
days—*clap own hands*
old—*clap partner's hands.*

Group Game

Invite children to stand in a circle. One child walks around the inside of the circle. The walking child taps a child in the circle on each musical beat but blows on children who come on musical rests. Those children go into the middle of the circle, which serves as the "porridge pot."

RING OUT THE OLD, RING IN THE NEW!

RELATED SONGS

Open, Shut Them

Traditional

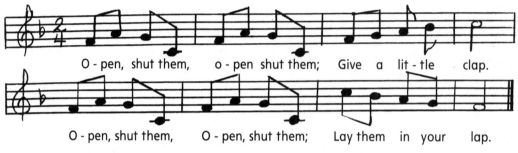

O - pen, shut them, o - pen shut them; Give a lit - tle clap.

O - pen, shut them, O - pen, shut them; Lay them in your lap.

This song involves the opposites *open* and *shut*.

Bounce High, Bounce Low

Folk Song, Adapted

Bounce high, bounce low; Bounce the ball to Shi - loh.

This song involves the opposites *high* and *low*.

Game

Children stand in a circle with the teacher in the middle. The teacher begins by bouncing the ball on each beat as he or she sings the song. On *Shiloh* the ball is bounced to a child, who repeats the song as he or she bounces the ball.

WINTER

RELATED PICTURE BOOKS

Bancroft, Henrietta. *Animals in Winter*. Crowell, 1963.
   A simple introduction to the habits of birds, bats, butterflies,
   and mammals in winter.

Borden, Louise. *Caps, Hats, Socks and Mittens*. Scholastic, 1989.
   Simple text and illustrations describe some of the pleasures
   of each season.

Brett, Jan. *The Mitten: A Ukrainian Folktale*. Putnam, 1989.
   Several animals sleep snugly in Nicki's lost mitten until the
   bear sneezes.

Briggs, Raymond. *The Snowman*. Random House, 1978.
   When his snowman comes to life, a little boy invites him
   home and in return is taken on a flight high above the
   countryside.

Bunting, Eve. *Red Fox Running*. Clarion Books, 1993.
   Rhyming text follows the experiences of a red fox as it
   searches across a wintry landscape for food.

Burningham, John. *The Snow*. Crowell, 1975.
   A boy and his mother share snowy day activities.

Carlstrom, Nancy. *The Snow Speaks*. Little, Brown, 1992.
   Captures the sights and sounds of the season's first snowfall.

Craft, Ruth. *The Winter Bear*. Atheneum, 1975.
   Recounts in rhyme the adventures of three children out on
   a winter's walk.

Delton, Judy. *A Walk on a Snowy Night*. Harper & Row, 1982.
   A walk on a snowy night brings a little girl and her father
   closer together.

Frost, Robert. *Stopping by Woods on a Snowy Evening*. Dutton, 1978.
   Illustrations of wintry scenes accompany each line of the
   well-known poem.

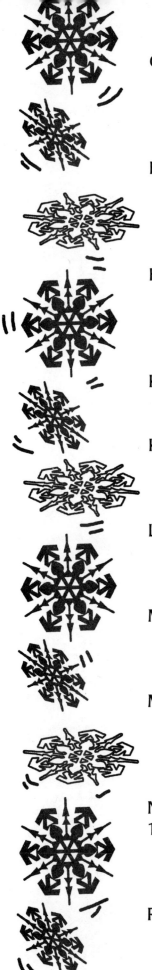

Goffstein, M. B. *Our Snowman*. Harper & Row, 1986.
The snowman two children builds looks so lonely when night comes that the little girl and her father go out and make a snowman to keep him company.

Hader, Berta. *The Big Snow*. Macmillan, 1948.
Despite their elaborate preparations for the winter, the animals and birds are delighted by a surprise banquet after a big snow.

Hissey, Jane. *Jolly Snow*. Philomel Books, 1991.
Old Bear and his Friends wait for snow but when it doesn't come they make a blizzard of snow in the house with flour, with bubbles and with feathers.

Keats, Ezra Jack. *The Snowy Day*. Viking, 1962.
The adventures of a little boy in the city on a very snowy day.

Killer, Holly. *Geraldine's Big Snow*. Greenwillow Books, 1988.
Geraldine can't wait for the snow to come so that she can coast down the hill on her sled.

Lobe, Mira. *The Snowman Who Went for a Walk*. Morrow, 1984.
A snowman becomes mobile, and in his wanderings decides to seek a place where he can live and never melt.

McCully, Emily. *First Snow*. Harper & Row, 1985.
A timid little mouse discovers the thrill of sledding in the first snow of the winter. Wordless.

Munsch, Robert. *Thomas' Snowsuit*. Annick Press, 1985.
Thomas will not wear his ugly new snowsuit and his mother, the teacher, and the principal have a perfectly terrible time with it and their clothes too.

Neitzel, Shirley. *The Jacket I Wear in the Snow*. Greenwillow Books, 1989.
A young girl names all the clothes she must wear to play in the snow.

Roberts, Bethany. *Waiting-For-Spring Stories*. Harper & Row, 1984.
As the family passes the winter in their cozy home, Papa Rabbit tells them stories about other rabbits.

Rockwell, Anne and Harlow. ***The First Snowfall***. Macmillan, 1987.
A child enjoys the special sights and activities of a snow-covered world.

Rogers, Jean. ***Runaway Mittens***. Greenwillow Books, 1988.
Pica's mittens are always turning up in strange places, but when he finds them keeping the newborn puppies warm in their box, he decides to leave them where they are until spring. A story of an Eskimo boy.

Selsam, Millicent and Joyce Hunt. ***Keep Looking!*** Macmillan, 1988.
As the reader turns the page, a new animal is added to an illustration of a country home in the winter.

Tejima, Keizaburo. ***Fox's Dream***. Philomel Books, 1987.
Wandering through a winter forest, a lonely fox has an enchanting vision and then finds the companionship for which he has been longing.

Tresselt, Alvin. ***White Snow, Bright Snow***. Lothrop, Lee & Shepard, 1947.
When it begins to look, feel and smell like snow, everyone prepares for a winter blizzard.

Vincent, Gabrielle. ***Ernest and Celestine***. Greenwillow Books, 1982.
Ernest, a bear, and Celestine, a mouse, lose Celestine's stuffed bird in the snow.

Willard, Nancy. ***A Starlit Somersault Downhill***. Little, Brown, 1993.
Having made a plan with Bear to spend the winter napping in a cozy home, Rabbit finds himself too energetic to sleep and decides to join the world outside.

Zolotow, Charlotte. ***Something Is Going to Happen***. Harper & Row, 1988.
One by one, the members of a family awake one cold November morning to discover that during the night there has been a beautiful snowfall.

RELATED POEMS

Prelutsky, Jack, ed. **Read-Aloud Rhymes for the Very Young**. Alfred A. Knopf, 1986.
> "Dragon Smoke" by Lilian Moore, p. 74.
> "The More It Snows" by A. A. Milne, p. 74.
> "The Mitten Song" by Marie Louise Allen, p. 74.
> "Winter Sweetness" by Langston Hughes, p. 74.
> "Jack Frost" by Helen Bayley Davis, p. 75.
> "It Fell in the City" by Eve Merriam, p. 75.
> "First Snow" by Marie Louise Allen, p. 76.
> "Icy" by Rhoda W. Bacmeister, p. 76.
> "January" by Maurice Sendak, p. 76.
> "Snowman" by David McCord, p. 77.
> "Snow" by Karla Kuskin, p. 77.

Sing a Song of Popcorn. Scholastic, 1988.
> "Furry Bear" by A. A. Milne, p. 22.
> "Snow" by Issa, p. 133.

TOYS ON PARADE

RELATED PICTURE BOOKS

Ashforth, Camilla. **Monkey Tricks**. Candlewick Press, 1992.
> While his friend Horatio, a stuffed rabbit, enjoys the bungled tricks of a mischievous monkey, James, a teddy bear, wonders why the props look so familiar.

Brown, Ruth. **I Don't Like It!** Dutton, 1989.
> When a little girl gets a puppy, her rag doll feels lonely and forgotten, but the girl's other toys don't mind. The doll seems to be the only one who wants some fun until puppy himself turns up to play.

Butler, Dorothy. **My Brown Bear Barney**. Greenwillow Books, 1988.
> On her many travels, a small girl takes many things, especially her brown bear, Barney.

Dodds, Doyle. **Wheel Away!** Harper & Row, 1989.
> A runaway wheel takes a bouncy, bumpy, amusing journey through town.

Douglass, Barbara. **Good As New**. Lothrop, Lee & Shepard, 1982.
When Grady's young cousin ruins his teddy bear, Grandpa promises to fix the toy.

Freeman, Don. **Beady Bear**. Viking Press, 1954.
A wind-up toy bear has adventures on a snowy night.

Freeman, Don. **Corduroy**. Viking Press, 1968.
A toy bear in a department store wants a number of things, but when a little girl finally buys him he finds what he has always wanted most of all.

Hague, Kathleen. **Alphabears: An ABC Book**. Holt, Rinehart & Winston, 1984.
Introduces a bear for each letter of the alphabet and describes its special qualities in rhyme.

Hague, Michael. **Teddy Bear, Teddy Bear: A Classic Action Rhyme**. Morrow, 1993.
An illustrated version of the traditional rhyme that follows the activities of a teddy bear.

Hayes, Sarah. **This Is the Bear**. Lippincott, 1986.
A toy bear is accidentally taken to the dump but is rescued by a boy and a dog.

Hissey, Jane. **Old Bear**. Philomel Books, 1986.
A group of toy animals try various ways of rescuing Old Bear from the attic.

Hissey, Jane. **Little Bear's Trousers**. Philomel Books, 1987.
While looking for his missing trousers, Little Bear discovers that other animals have found many different uses for them.

Kroll, Steven. **The Hand-Me-Down-Doll**. The Holiday House, 1983.
A lonely doll without a name endures a series of terrible misfortunes before she finally finds someone to love her.

Lionni, Leo. **Alexander and the Wind-Up Mouse**. Alfred A. Knopf, 1974.
Alexander, a real mouse, wants to be a toy mouse like his friend, Willy, until he discovers Willy is to be thrown away.

Young, Ruth. **Golden Bear**. Viking, 1992.
Golden Bear and his human companion learn to play the violin, talk to a ladybug, make mudpies, wish on stars, and dream together.

Zolotow, Charlotte. **William's Doll**. Harper & Row, 1972.
William's father gives him a basketball and a train but these do not make him want a doll any less.

RELATED POEMS

Prelutsky, Jack, ed. **Read-Aloud Rhymes for the Very Young**. Alfred A. Knopf, 1986.
"My Teddy Bear" by Marchette Chute, p. 53.
"My Teddy Bear" by Margaret Hillert, p. 53.

RING OUT THE OLD, RING IN THE NEW!

RELATED PICTURE BOOKS (OLD AND NEW)

Bolognese, Don. **A New Day**. Delacorte Press, 1970.
The birth of a son to a migrant couple in a garage attracts such joyful attention that the police plan to arrest the parents for disturbing the peace. This is a modern-day Nativity tale.

Burton, Virginia Lee. **Mike Mulligan and His Steam Shovel**. Houghton Mifflin, 1939.
When Mike Mulligan and his steam shovel, Mary Ann, lose their jobs to the gasoline, electric and diesel motor shovels, they go to a little country town where they find that one new job leads to another.

DePaola, Tomie. **Charlie Needs a Cloak**. Prentice-Hall, 1974.
A shepherd shears his sheep, cards and spins the wool, weaves and dyes the cloth, and sews a beautiful new red cloak.

Herriot, James. **_Moses the Kitten_**. St. Martin's Press, 1984.
A bedraggled, orphaned kitten is nursed back to health on a Yorkshire farm. When he recovers, he has a very unusual idea about the identity of his mother.

Sharmat, Marjorie. **_Griselda's New Year_**. Macmillan, 1979.
Griselda Goose attempts to carry out her New Year's resolutions, but her good deeds backfire.

Stevenson, James. **_The Night After Christmas_**. Greenwillow Books, 1981.
Tossed in garbage cans after they are replaced by new toys at Christmas, a teddy bear and a doll are befriended by a stray dog.

Wells, Rosemary. **_Peabody_**. Dial Books, 1983.
Annie's affection for Peabody, her teddy bear, is temporarily overshadowed by the novelty of a new talking birthday doll.

Williams, Margery. **_The Velveteen Rabbit_**. Derrydale Books, 1986.
By the time the velveteen rabbit is dirty, worn out, and about to be burned, he has almost given up hope of ever finding the magic called Real.

Ziefert, Harriet. **_A New Coat for Anna_**. Alfred A. Knopf, 1986.
Even though there is no money, Anna's mother finds a way to make Anna a badly needed winter coat.

RELATED PICTURE BOOKS (OPPOSITES)

Allington, Richard. **_Beginning to Learn about Opposites_**. Raintree Children's Books, 1979.
Introduces 14 pairs of opposites, such as big and little, same and different, along with the concept that the same object can be its own opposite, depending upon perspective.

Burningham, John. **_John Burningham's Opposites_**. Crown Publishing.
Introduces the concept of opposites through labeled pictures of a boy interacting with a thin pig and fat pig, a hot dragon and a cold snowman, and other creatures and situations.

Cuyler, Margery. ***That's Good! That's Bad!*** Henry Holt, 1991.
A little boy has a series of adventures and misadventures with a bunch of wild animals.

Gillham, Bill and Susan Hulme. ***Let's Look for Opposites***. Coward-McCann, 1984.
Illustrates such opposite concepts as full/empty, open/shut, top/bottom, and dark/light, using photographs and sentences.

Hoban, Tana. ***Exactly the Opposite***. Greenwillow Books, 1990.
Photographs of familiar outdoor scenes illustrate pairs of opposites.

Hoban, Tana. ***Push, Pull, Empty, Full: A Book of Opposites***. Macmillan, 1972.
Black-and-white photos illustrate fifteen pairs of opposites, such as front/back, first/last, push/pull.

Maestro, Betsy and Giulio. ***Traffic: A Book of Opposites***. Crown Publishing, 1981.
Text and illustrations introduce words with opposite meanings, such as over and under, big and little, and front and back.

McMillan, Bruce. ***Becca Backward, Becca Frontward: A Book of Opposites***. Lothrop, Lee & Shepard, 1986.
Photographs of a girl involved in various activities illustrate such opposite concepts as above/below, full/empty, and big/small.

McMillan, Bruce. ***Dry or Wet?*** Lothrop, Lee & Shepard, 1988.
Paired photographs illustrate the concepts of wet and dry.

McMillan, Bruce. ***Here a Chick, There a Chick***. Lothrop, Lee & Shepard, 1983.
Photographs of baby chicks are used to illustrate such opposite concepts as inside/outside, asleep/awake, and alone/together.

Mendoza, George. ***Sesame Street Book of Opposites with Zero Mostel***. Platt & Munk, 1974.
Zero Mostel portrays in pantomime the difference between such opposites as on/off, nice/grouchy, yummy/yucchy, and light/heavy.

FEBRUARY

First Year

FRIENDSHIP PATCHWORK

Objectives

- Children will learn to classify various fabrics according to color, design, hue, and texture.
- Children will feel a sense of group unity.
- Children will take part in group decision making.
- Children will practice friendship skills.

Second Year

ANIMALS ARE OUR FRIENDS

Objectives

- Children will learn about pet responsibility.
- Children will learn how birds and animals survive the winter.
- Children will learn compassion for animals.

COMMENTARY

Friendships

At three years of age, friends become extremely important to children. By three-and-a-half, children are able to play cooperatively. They are learning about sharing, taking turns, and asking for what they want rather than just taking it. However, a parent or teacher should be nearby in order to help children settle their disputes.

Four-year-olds especially enjoy being with friends and having a special friend. They play with both boys and girls but their best friend is usually of the same sex. At this age, there may be much name-calling, quarreling, and sometimes, hitting. Children are learning to resolve their quarrels and disputes but need an adult nearby to help them.

At five, children improve at taking turns. Since their sense of property is developing, they are also learning to respect the belongings of others and to ask permission to use things. Five-year-olds play better with just one other child or in small groups of five to six children.

In the early primary grades, there is much rough-and-tumble play on the school playground. Children may shout at each other and fight for their rights. Each child wants to be "first," "leader," or "winner" in whatever game he or she is playing. Children may need to be taught all over again about taking turns and getting along.

Throughout the year, it is helpful to read books about friendships. These can lead to discussions about how the boys and girls in the stories resolve their conflicts. Children can be taught friendship skills, such as introducing oneself to a new friend or asking a child if he or she wants to play. The teacher might wish to demonstrate the skills with puppets. Children may use puppets to practice the skills that are taught.

The theme **Friendship Patchwork** is designed to help children increase their sense of group unity. *The Rag Coat* by Lauren Mills is a good book to read, since it is about both friendship and patchwork.

References

Jenkins, Gladys G. and Helen S. Schacter. *These Are Your Children*. Scott, Foresman, 1975.

Ames, Louise Bates and Frances L. Ilg. *Your Three Year Old*. Gesell Institute of Child Development, 1976 (a series of books about each year in a young child's life).

FRIENDSHIP PATCHWORK

LETTER TO PARENTS

Dear Family:

As a cooperative project this month, we will be making a patchwork in conjunction with our theme, **Friendship Patchwork**. For your child's sharing time, please contribute four or five 6" x 6" (15 cm x 15 cm) squares of fabric. The squares may be from one large piece of fabric or they may be an assortment. Your child will tell us where the scraps came from—a baby blanket, Halloween costume, trip to a fabric shop, Grandma's attic, or wherever. Children will be examining and sorting the fabrics in various ways, such as by color, design, hue, or texture. When the month is over, we will ask volunteers to sew the pieces together. We will decide as a group what to make with our patchwork. Perhaps it will be a curtain, a pillow slip, a quilt, or even a "remembrance skirt" for a teacher.

We will read many books about friendships this month. We will ask the children about their friends as well—what do their friends do that they like or dislike? What do they do that their friends like or dislike? We will also talk about ways to help friends. Children and teachers will use puppets to illustrate and practice friendship skills.

On your child's sharing day, please send in valentines for all your child's classmates. The most special valentines are those the children make themselves. Children may enjoy working on them at home this month.

Sincerely,

Your Child's Teachers

ANIMALS ARE OUR FRIENDS
LETTER TO PARENTS

Dear Family:

Your child's pet is invited for a short visit this month to help celebrate our theme, **Animals Are Our Friends**. For sharing time, your child may tell us how he or she shares responsibility for the pet and give some information about pet care. Alternatively, your child may bring a stuffed toy, drawing, or picture of a favorite animal.

A caretaker from the animal shelter will talk to the children about pet responsibility. In addition, we will learn how animals survive the winter. We wish to promote feelings of compassion for all animals—particularly those that must endure winter's hardships.

For Valentine's Day, children will make valentines for the birds. On sharing day, your child may bring valentines for everyone.

Sincerely,

Your Child's Teachers

116

SUGGESTED ACTIVITIES FOR FEBRUARY

COOKING PROJECTS

Cooperative Soup

Ask children to bring in a plastic zipper bag full of 1" (2.5 cm) pieces of raw vegetables, such as carrots, potatoes, celery, or tomatoes. Encourage them to help scrub the vegetables at home. Read *Stone Soup* by Marcia Brown to the class. Invite children to dramatize the story as they contribute their vegetables to the soup. You may wish to use a broth powder or soup starter for the base. Quick-cooking barley or alphabet noodles may also be added to the soup. Compare the difference between the raw and cooked vegetables with children.

Valentine Treats

Provide mini-bagels and soft strawberry cream cheese for children to spread with a tongue depressor or plastic knife. If strawberries are available in your area of the country, cut some into heart shapes by slicing them in half lengthwise and removing the stem portion. Invite children to place strawberry hearts in the center of their bagels after they have spread the cream cheese.

ARTS AND CRAFTS PROJECTS

Valentine Mice

Help children cut out one large and one tiny heart from pink or red construction paper. The large heart is kept folded for the mouse's body and the small heart is glued in place for ears. A pink or red yarn tail may be added. Show children how to draw whiskers and eyes with a fine-tipped marker.

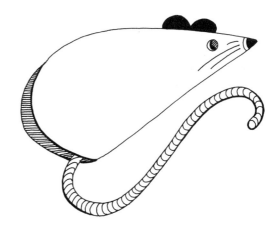

Valentine Collages

Invite children to choose lilac, pink, or red cardstock to use as their collage backgrounds. Give each child an Ellison heart shape and a heart outline cut from floral wallpaper. Provide an assortment of collage materials, such as doilies, lace, ribbons, pink or white buttons, and yarn, for children to add. Display finished collages at your Valentine party.

117

ADDITIONAL IDEAS AND PROJECTS

Valentine Exchange

Children may bring valentines on their sharing day to distribute at the end of story time. Children might bring their valentines home each day or keep them in a special valentine mailbox.

Valentine Party

- Read Eric Carle's *Do You Want to Be My Friend?*; *Mr. Griggs' Work* by Cynthia Rylant; *Somebody Loves You, Mr. Hatch* by Eileen Spinelli; or *The Jolly Postman* by Janet Ahlberg.

- Invite the mail carrier to visit the classroom during his or her regular rounds and give the carrier a valentine from the class. Ask the letter carrier to describe briefly the job.

- Offer the letter carrier a valentine mini-bagel and some pink lemonade.

- Help children make Hershey's Kiss™ or Hug™ mice by gluing the flat bottoms of Kisses or Hugs to both sides of pink construction-paper hearts. Encourage children to press the glued candies together against the hearts with both hands as they count to ten *slowly* while the glue dries. The lobes of the hearts appear as ears between the candy head and body while the paper "tail" protrudes from one end. Add plastic jiggle eyes at the other end if appropriate for your students.

- Sing game songs, such as "A Tisket, A Tasket," "Little Sally Waters," "Ida Red," "Old Brass Wagon," "Skip to My Lou," or "Love Somebody," at the party (see pages 120–124).

FRIENDSHIP PATCHWORK

ARTS & CRAFTS PROJECTS

Paper Patchwork

Give each child a 9" (22.5 cm) square of white or light-colored construction paper. Invite children to draw themselves and a friend doing something they both enjoy with crayons or markers. Display the finished illustrations on a bulletin board in several rows alternating with red or pink 9" construction paper squares—a paper friendship patchwork.

Friendship Puzzles

Invite children to work with partners on a puzzle project. Give each pair of children a plastic zipper bag and a sheet of white construction paper on which to draw a picture of friends doing something together. Discuss with children that friends can be older or younger relatives or children, animals, or their peers. Help children cut finished illustrations into five or six puzzle pieces and seal them in the zipper bags. Children will exchange puzzles with other pairs of students. Encourage each pair to work together to reassemble the new puzzles.

ANIMALS ARE OUR FRIENDS

ARTS & CRAFTS PROJECTS

Pet-ting Zoo

Create a display entitled "Pet-ting Zoo" on a bulletin board. Invite children to draw their pets or the pets they would like to have. Encourage them to add background details that tell a bit about the animal's environment. Children may wish to include themselves in their illustrations. Help children write the animals' names on their illustrations before displaying them in the "zoo."

Birds' Valentines

Help children press heart-shaped cookie cutters into slices of white bread. Show them how to brush the bread hearts with egg white and sprinkle with bird seed. When the bread is partially dry, thread a strand of red curling ribbon through the bread for hanging. If you have a tree outside a classroom window, hang the valentine treats outside for birds to enjoy.

The More We Are Together

Camp Song

The more we are to-geth-er, to-geth-er, to-geth-er,

The more we are to-geth-er, the hap-pier we'll be,

For your friends are my friends and my friends are

your friends, The more we are to-geth-er, the

hap-pier we'll be.

FEATURED BOOK

Spinelli, Eileen. ***Somebody Loves You, Mr. Hatch***. Bradbury Press, 1991.

An anonymous valentine changes the life of the unsociable Mr. Hatch, turning him into a laughing friend who helps and appreciates all his neighbors.

FRIENDSHIP PATCHWORK

RELATED SONGS

A Tisket, A Tasket **Traditional**

A tis-ket, a tas-ket,

A green and yel-low bas-ket,

I sent a let-ter to my love

And on the way I dropped it,

I dropped it.

Game

Have children stand in a circle. One child walks around the outside of the circle with a letter in one hand. At the words, "I dropped it," the walking child drops the letter behind a child in the circle. (The words *I dropped it* may be repeated until a child is chosen.) When a child gets a letter dropped behind him or her, that child chases and tries to catch the other child, who is running around the circle trying to reach the empty spot. If the runner is tagged, he or she must try again by dropping the letter behind a different child. If the runner makes it to the empty spot untagged, the former occupant of that spot takes the letter and becomes the walker.

Love Somebody **American Folk Song**

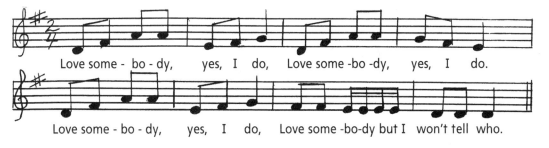

Love some-bo-dy, yes, I do, Love some-bo-dy, yes, I do.

Love some-bo-dy, yes, I do, Love some-bo-dy but I won't tell who.

RELATED SONGS

Skidamarink

Skid - a - ma - rink a dink - a - dink, skid - a - ma - rink a doo, I love you. Skid - a - ma - rink a dink - a - dink, skid - a - ma - rink a doo, I love you. I love you in the morn - ing and in the af - ter - noon, I love you in the eve - ning and un - der - neath the moon, Oh, skid - a - ma - rink a dink - a - dink skid - a - ma - rink a doo, I love you!

Actions

Skidamarink-a-dinkadink *(put right elbow in left hand and wiggle fingers)*
  Skidamarink-a-doo. *(repeat, using opposite elbow and hand)*
I *(point to self)* love *(hug self)* you *(point to other person)*.
I love you in the morning *(put hand up high)* and in the afternoon
  (put hand at shoulder level).
I love you in the evening *(put hand at hip level)* and underneath the
  moon *(make big circle with arms)*.
Oh, skidamarink-a-dinkadink,
Skidamarink-a-doo,
I love you *(same motions as first two lines)*.

FRIENDSHIP PATCHWORK

RELATED SONGS

Little Sally Waters
Traditional Game Song

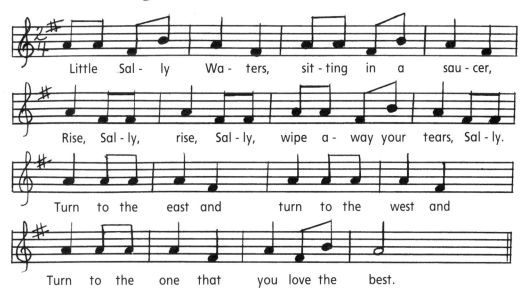

Little Sal - ly Wa - ters, sit - ting in a sau - cer,

Rise, Sal - ly, rise, Sal - ly, wipe a - way your tears, Sal - ly.

Turn to the east and turn to the west and

Turn to the one that you love the best.

Game

Have children make a circle by joining hands. One child stands in the center, covering eyes with both hands. As the song is sung, children move around the circle as the child in the center acts out the words to the song. At the end of the song, with eyes still covered, the center child points to another child, who then becomes the new "Sally." The song is repeated.

Aliki. *We Are Best Friends*. Greenwillow Books, 1982.

When Robert's best friend, Peter, moves away, both are unhappy but they learn that they can make new friends and still remain best friends.

FRIENDSHIP PATCHWORK

RELATED SONGS

Ida Red
Traditional

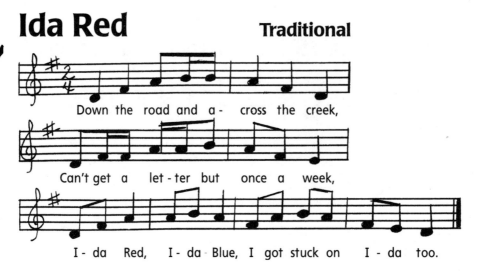

Down the road and a - cross the creek,

Can't get a let - ter but once a week,

I - da Red, I - da Blue, I got stuck on I - da too.

Game
Have children make a circle. One child with a letter in hand walks or skips around the circle until he or she drops the letter behind another child at the end of the song. That child chases the first around the circle, trying to get back to the empty space.

Old Brass Wagon
Traditional

Cir - cle to the left, old brass wa - gon;

Cir - cle to the left, old brass wa - gon;

Cir - cle to the left, old brass wa - gon;

You're the one my dar - ling.

Other verses:

2. Circle to the right.

3. Everybody in.

4. Everybody out.

Encourage children to make up new action verses.

ANIMALS ARE OUR FRIENDS

RELATED SONGS

The North Wind Doth Blow
Mother Goose

The north wind doth blow— and we shall have snow, And what will poor Ro - bin do then, poor thing? He'll sit in a barn— and keep him - self warm and hide his head un - der his wing, poor thing!

2. The north wind doth blow,
   And we shall have snow,
   And what will the dormouse do then, poor thing?
   Rolled up in a ball,
   In his nest snug and small,
   He'll sleep 'til warm weather comes in, poor thing.

Hader, Berta and Elmer. ***The Big Snow***. Collier Books, 1948.

Story of the little old man and woman who lived in the only house on the hillside and how, during the long, cold winter, they put out pans of food and scattered seeds and corn which fed animals and birds and kept them alive until spring.

ANIMALS ARE OUR FRIENDS

RELATED SONGS

Wild Bird

Japanese Singing Game

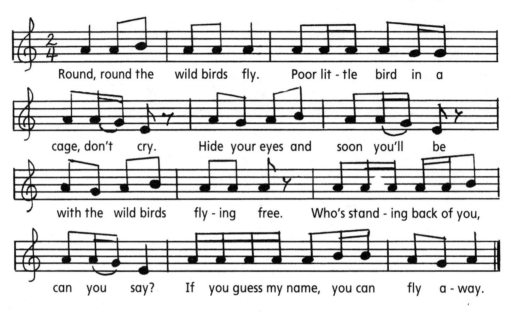

Round, round the wild birds fly. Poor lit-tle bird in a cage, don't cry. Hide your eyes and soon you'll be with the wild birds fly-ing free. Who's stand-ing back of you, can you say? If you guess my name, you can fly a-way.

Invite children to hold hands and circle around a child in the middle, who has his or her eyes closed. On the word *free*, everyone stops circling. Whoever is standing directly behind the child in the middle is the one who sings, "If you guess my name, you can fly away." If the child in the middle can identify the singing voice, the two children exchange places and the game continues.

FEATURED BOOK

Watts, Bernadette. *St. Francis and the Proud Crow*. Orchard Books, 1987.

After St. Francis grants his wish for a golden cage, Crow realizes the folly of envy and the value of freedom and love.

ANIMALS ARE OUR FRIENDS

I Love Little Pussy

Mother Goose

I— love lit-tle pus-sy, her coat is so warm, And—
if I don't hurt her she'll do me no harm. I'll—
sit by the fire— and give her some food, And—
pus-sy will love me be-cause I am good.

Hey my kitten, my kitten
And hey my kitten, my deary,
Such a sweet pet as this
There is not far nor neary.

      – Mother Goose

Diddledy, diddledy, dumpty,
The cat ran up the plum tree.
Half a crown to fetch her down,
Diddledy, diddledy, dumpty.

      – Mother Goose

127

RELATED SONGS

Rover

Traditional English Song

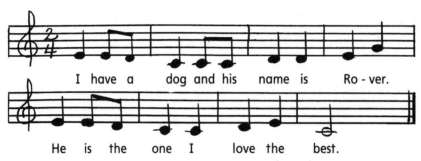

I have a dog and his name is Ro-ver.

He is the one I love the best.

2. When he is good he is good all over.
   When he is bad, he is a pest.

Bow wow wow. Who's dog art thou?
Little Tommy Tinker's dog. Bow wow wow.

— *Mother Goose*

Oh where, oh where has my little dog gone?
Oh where, oh where can he be?
With his ears cut short
And his tail cut long,
Oh where, oh where can he be?

— *Mother Goose*

FEATURED BOOK

Sharmat, Marjorie Weinman. ***I'm the Best!***
Holiday House, 1991.

A dog who has lived with many owners
and has had many different names finally
finds the family that wants to keep him
and love him forever.

ANIMALS ARE OUR FRIENDS

RELATED SONGS

Nibble, Nibble, Nibble
Words by Margaret Wise Brown
Melody by Karen Medley

Nib - ble, nib - ble, nib - ble, goes the mouse in my heart.

Nib - ble, nib - ble, nib - ble, goes the mouse in my heart.

Nib -ble, nib - ble, nib - ble, goes the mouse in my heart, and the

mouse in my heart is you!

2. Hippety, hippety hop goes the bunny in my heart *(repeat three times)*
   And the bunny in my heart is you!
3. Flippity, flippity flop goes the fish in my heart *(repeat three times)*
   And the fish in my heart is you!
4. Softly now goes the beating of my heart *(repeat three times)*
   All for the love of you!

From *Nibble, Nibble, Nibble* by Karen Medley and Margaret Wise Brown. Young Scott Books. Out of print. Used by permission.

FEATURED BOOK

Carle, Eric. ***Do You Want to Be My Friend?*** Crowell, 1971.

A mouse searches everywhere for a friend.

FRIENDSHIP PATCHWORK

RELATED PICTURE BOOKS

Alexander, Martha. *Blackboard Bear*. Dial Books, 1969.
Pictures and brief text show how an imaginative little
boy gets even with the big boys who won't let him
play with them.

Aliki. *At Mary Bloom's*. Greenwillow Books, 1976.
What happens at Mary Bloom's when her friend's mouse
has babies.

Aliki. *We Are Best Friends*. Greenwillow Books, 1982.
When Robert's best friend, Peter, moves away, both are
unhappy but they learn that they can make new friends
and still remain best friends.

Brandenberg, Franz. *Nice New Neighbors*. Greenwillow Books, 1977.
The fieldmouse children find a way to make new friends
when they move to a new house.

Cannon, Janell. *Stellaluna*. Harcourt Brace Jovanovich, 1993.
After she falls headfirst into a bird's nest, a baby bat is
raised like a bird until she is reunited with her mother.

Carlstrom, Nancy White. *Fish and Flamingo*. Little, Brown, 1993.
Two unlikely friends, Fish and Flamingo, spend time
together, help each other out, and tell stories about
their different lives.

Charlip, Remy. *Harlequin and the Gift of Many Colors*. Parent's
Magazine Press, 1973.
Due to the generosity of his friends, Harlequin gets a new
patchwork suit for Carnival.

Cohen, Miriam. *Best Friends*. Macmillan, 1971.
When the light in the classroom incubator burns out, two
friends are brought together again as they act to save the
lives of the unhatched chickens.

Delacre, Lulu. ***Nathan and Nicholas Alexander***. Scholastic, 1986.
The story of how a mouse and an elephant make friends and share a room.

Delton, Judy. ***Two Good Friends***. Crown Publishing, 1974.
A warm friendship develops between an unlikely pair—an immaculate Duck and a slovenly Bear. Duck tidies up for his messy friend and Bear, who's a master chef, reciprocates with delicious pastries.

Foreman, Michael. ***The Two Giants***. Pantheon Books, 1967.
A pink sea shell leads two giants to a terrible argument that lasts for years and is finally resolved when the giants realize they have mixed their socks.

Fox, Mem. ***Wilfrid Gordon McDonald Partridge***. Kane/Miller, 1985.
A small boy tries to discover the meaning of "memory" so he can restore that of an elderly friend.

Hallinan, P.K. ***That's What a Friend Is***. Childrens Press, 1977.
Describes friendship in rhymed text and illustrations.

Havill, Juanita. ***Jamaica's Find***. Houghton Mifflin, 1986.
A little girl finds a stuffed dog in the park and decides to take it home.

Havill, Juanita. ***Jamaica Tag-Along***. Houghton Mifflin, 1989.
When her older brother refuses to let her tag along with him, Jamaica goes off by herself and allows a younger child to play with her.

Hayes, Geoffrey. ***Patrick and Ted***. Four Winds Press, 1984.
Best friends, Patrick and Ted, find their relationship strained when Ted goes away for the summer and Patrick finds other activities and friends to occupy his time.

Henkes, Kevin. ***Chester's Way***. Greenwillow Books, 1988.
Chester and Wilson share the same exact way of doing things, until Lilly moves into the neighborhood and shows them that new ways can be just as good.

Henkes, Kevin. ***Jessica***. Greenwillow Books, 1989.
  Ruthie does everything with her imaginary friend Jessica.
  Then, on her first day of kindergarten, she meets a real new
  friend with the same name.

Hughes, Shirley. ***Alfie Gives a Hand***. Lothrop, Lee & Shepard, 1983.
  Holding tightly his old bit of blanket as he attends his first
  birthday party, Alfie finds a way to be helpful, but it means
  putting down his blanket first.

Hutchins, Pat. ***My Best Friend***. Greenwillow Books, 1993.
  Despite differences in abilities, two little girls appreciate
  each other and are "best friends."

Iwasaki, Chihiro. ***Will You Be My Friend?*** McGraw-Hill, 1973.
  Allison is just about to ask the new boy moving in next
  door to be her friend when the trouble begins.

Jewell, Nancy. ***Cheer Up, Pig!*** Harper & Row, 1975.
  Pig discovers that sometimes it's nice to have friends
  around and sometimes it's nice to be alone.

Joosse, Barbara. ***Better with Two***. Harper & Row, 1988.
  Laura tries to make Mrs. Brody feel better when her dog
  Max dies.

Kasza, Keiko. ***The Rat and the Tiger***. G.P. Putnam's Sons, 1993.
  In his friendship with Rat, Tiger takes advantage and plays
  the bully because of his greater size, but one day Rat stands
  up for his rights.

Lillie, Patricia. ***Jake and Rosie***. Greenwillow Books, 1989.
  Jake is upset not to find his best friend Rosie at home, but
  Rosie soon returns and shows Jake a nice surprise.

Marshall, James. ***George and Martha***. Houghton Mifflin, 1972.
Marshall, James. ***George and Martha, Back in Town***. Houghton
Mifflin, 1984.
Marshall, James. ***One Fine Day***. Houghton Mifflin, 1978.
  Several episodes in the friendship of two hippopotamuses.

Mills, Lauren. ***The Rag Coat***. Little, Brown, 1991.
   Minna proudly wears her new coat made of clothing scraps
   to school, where the other children laugh at her until she
   tells them the stories behind her scraps.

Morris, Ann. ***Loving***. Lothrop, Lee & Shepard, 1990.
   Examples of the different ways in which love can be
   expressed with an emphasis on the relationship between
   parent and child.

Polacco, Patricia. ***Mrs. Katz and Tush***. Bantam Books, 1992.
   A long-lasting friendship develops between Larnel, a young
   African-American and Mrs. Katz, a lonely Jewish widow, when
   Larnel presents Mrs. Katz a scrawny kitten without a tail.

Rogers, Fred. ***Making Friends***. G. P. Putnam's Sons, 1987.
   Explains what it means to be friends and some of the easy
   and difficult aspects of friendship.

Rosenberg, Maxine. ***My Friend Leslie: The Story of a Handicapped
Child***. Lothrop, Lee & Shepard, 1983.
   Presents a multi-handicapped kindergarten child, who is
   well-accepted by her classmates, in various situations within
   the school setting.

Ross, Dave. ***A Book of Hugs***. Crowell, 1980.
   Describes a variety of hugs, including people hugs, blanket
   hugs, and birthday hugs, and presents facts and hints about
   hugs.

Spinelli, Eileen. ***Somebody Loves You, Mr. Hatch***. Bradbury Press, 1991.
   An anonymous valentine changes the life of the unsociable
   Mr. Hatch, turning him into a laughing friend who helps and
   appreciates all his neighbors.

Stevenson, James. ***Wilfred the Rat***. Greenwillow Books, 1977.
   A lonely rat is befriended by a chipmunk and squirrel at an
   amusement park and when his fortunes change he must
   decide how important that friendship is.

Stren, Patti. ***Hug Me***. Harper & Row, 1977.
   A porcupine wants a friend to hug more than anything else
   in the world.

Vincent, Gabrielle. ***Ernest and Celestine's Patchwork Quilt***. Greenwillow Books, 1982.

> Ernest and Celestine make a patchwork quilt, but when they realize only one can use it, they make another one.

Viorst, Judith. ***Rosie and Michael***. Atheneum, 1974.

> Two friends tell what they like about each other—even the bad things.

Waber, Bernard. ***Ira Sleeps Over***. Houghton Mifflin, 1972.

> A little boy is excited at the prospect of spending the night at his friend's house but worries how he'll get along without his teddy bear.

Wagner, Jenny. ***John Brown, Rose and the Midnight Cat***. Puffin Books, 1980.

> Rose's dog feels he can look after her without any help from a cat, but Rose has different ideas.

Wells, Rosemary. ***Timothy Goes to School***. Dial Books, 1981.

> Timothy learns about being accepted and making friends during the first week of his first year at school.

Wittman, Sally. ***A Special Trade***. Harper & Row, 1978.

> As the years go by, a little girl is able to help an old man as he helped her when she was very young.

Zolotow, Charlotte. ***I Know a Lady***. Greenwillow Books, 1984.

> Sally describes a loving and lovable old lady in her neighborhood who grows flowers, waves to children when they pass her house, and bakes cookies for them at Christmas.

Zolotow, Charlotte. ***My Friend John***. Harper & Row, 1968.

> John's best friend tells everything he knows about John, the secrets they share, their likes and dislikes, and the fun they have as friends.

Zolotow, Charlotte. ***The Hating Book***. Harper & Row, 1969.

> A little girl knew her friend hated her but she didn't ask why until she finally got up courage to ask why they were being so rotten to each other.

ANIMALS ARE OUR FRIENDS

RELATED PICTURE BOOKS

Abercrombie, Barbara. ***Charlie Anderson***. Margaret K. McElderry Books, 1990.
> A cat comes out of the night to steal the hearts of two sisters who look forward to his sleeping on their beds until one day, Charlie doesn't come home and they learn a surprising secret about him.

Asch, Frank. ***The Last Puppy***. Simon & Schuster, 1989.
> The last born of nine puppies worries that he will be the last chosen for a pet of a new owner.

Balian, Lorna. ***Amelia's Nine Lives***. Abingdon Press, 1986.
> Nine of Nora's friends and relatives bring her replacement cats after she loses her beloved Amelia, but there is still one surprise in store.

Bancroft, Henrietta. ***Animals in Winter***. Crowell, 1963.
> A simple introduction to the habits of birds, bats, butterflies, and mammals in winter.

Brett, Jan. ***Annie and the Wild Animals***. Houghton Mifflin, 1985.
> When Annie's cat disappears, she attempts friendship with a variety of unsuitable woodland animals, but with the emergence of spring, everything comes right.

Brown, Margaret Wise. ***The Dead Bird***. HarperCollins, 1958.
> In finding a dead bird that is still warm, a little girl and her playmates meet death for the first time.

Carle, Eric. ***Do You Want to Be My Friend?*** Crowell, 1971.
> A mouse searches everywhere for a friend.

Carrick, Carol. ***Lost in the Storm***. Clarion Books, 1974.
> Christopher must wait out a long, fretful night before searching for his dog lost during an island storm.

Chalmers, Mary. ***Six Dogs, Twenty-Three Cats, Forty-Five Mice and One Hundred Sixteen Spiders***. Harper & Row, 1986.
> Annie tries unsuccessfully to keep her 190 pets out of the company room to avoid frightening her friend, Priscilla.

Cherry, Lynne. ***Archie, Follow Me***. Dutton Children's Books, 1990.
A little girl describes her relationship with her cat.

Daugherty, James. ***Andy and the Lion***. Viking Press, 1938.
In this retelling of Androcles and the Lion, Andy meets a lion on the way to school and wins his friendship for life by removing a thorn from his paw.

Day, Alexandra. ***Carl Goes Shopping***. Farrar, Straus & Giroux, 1989.
Carl the dog and a baby entertain each other in a department store.

DeRegniers, Beatrice Schenk. ***May I Bring a Friend?*** Atheneum, 1964.
A well-mannered little boy has permission to bring his animal friends to visit the king and queen.

Ets, Marie Hall. ***Play with Me***. Viking Press, 1955.
A little girl goes to the meadow to play but each animal she tries to catch runs away from her—until she sits still by the pond and they all come back.

Feder, Jane. ***Beany***. Pantheon Books, 1979.
A child describes his relationship to his cat.

Gackenbach, Dick. ***What's Claude Doing?*** Clarion Books, 1984.
A dog refuses all the neighborhood pets' invitations to come out to play, not admitting that he's generously keeping his sick master company.

Gomi. ***My Friends***. Chronicle Books, 1990.
A little girl learns to walk, climb, and study the earth from her friends, most of whom are animals.

Graham, Bob. ***Pete and Roland***. Viking Press, 1984.
Pete finds a sleepy blue parakeet in his backyard and enjoys keeping the bird as a pet until the day it decides to become independent again.

Hader, Berta and Elmer. ***The Big Snow***. Collier Books, 1948.
Story of the little old man and woman who lived in the only house on the hillside and how, during the long, cold winter, they put out pans of food and scattered seeds and corn which fed the animals and birds and kept them alive until spring.

Herriot, James. ***Moses the Kitten***. St. Martin's Press, 1984.
A bedraggled orphaned kitten is nursed back to health on a Yorkshire farm. When he recovers, he has a very unusual idea about the identity of his mother.

Johnson, Angela. ***Julius***. Orchard Books, 1993.
Maya's grandfather brings her a pig from Alaska and the two of them learn about fun and sharing together.

Keller, Holly. ***Furry***. Greenwillow Books, 1992.
Laura's allergies make it difficult for her to find a pet she likes, until her brother brings home a surprise.

Mazer, Anne. ***The Salamander Room***. Alfred A. Knopf, 1991.
A young boy finds a salamander and thinks of the many things he can do to make a perfect home for it. Relevant to ecology.

McPhail, David. ***Emma's Pet***. Dutton, 1985.
Emma's search for a soft cuddly pet has a surprising ending.

Mizumura, Kazue. ***If I Were a Cricket***. Crowell, 1973.
Short poems relate what small creatures could do to express their love.

Politi, Leo. ***Saint Francis and the Animals***. Charles Scribner's Sons, 1959.
Tells of St. Francis' friendship with various animals—birds, a little hare, doves, a pheasant, a fish, a lamb and the wolf of Gubbio.

Schweitzer, Byrd Baylor. ***Amigo***. Macmillan, 1963.
Desperately wanting a pet to love, a boy decides to tame a prairie dog who has already decided to tame the boy for his own pet.

Sharmat, Marjorie. ***I'm the Best***. Holiday House, 1991.
A dog who has lived with many owners and has had many different names finally finds the family that wants to keep him and love him forever.

Simon, Norma. ***Where Does My Cat Sleep?*** Albert Whitman, 1982.
At night each member of the family sleeps in his or her own bed but Rocky the cat sleeps anywhere and everywhere.

Turkle, Brinton. **Thy Friend, Obadiah**. Viking Press, 1969.
> A seagull befriends a Quaker boy, much to his embarrassment, and it is not until he has helped the bird that he can accept its friendship.

Turner, Dona. **My Cat Pearl**. Crowell, 1980.
> Describes the everyday activities of a pet cat and her young mistress.

Viorst, Judith. **The Tenth Good Thing about Barney**. Atheneum, 1971.
> The little boy in the story tries to think of ten good things to say about Barney (his recently-deceased cat) at the cat's funeral. With the gentle help of his parents, he is finally able to complete the list.

Watts, Bernadette. **St. Francis and the Proud Crow**. Orchard Books, 1987.
> After St. Francis grants his wish for a golden cage, Crow realizes the folly of envy and the value of freedom and love.

Wilhelm, Hans. **I'll Always Love You**. Crown Publishing, 1985.
> A child's sadness at the death of a beloved dog is tempered by the remembrance of saying to it every night, "I'll always love you."

Winch, Madeleine. **Come by Chance**. Crown Publishing, 1990.
> When Bertha finds an old tumbled-down house, she turns it into a cozy home and lives there by herself, until the stormy night when animals come seeking shelter from the rain.

RELATED POETRY

Prelutsky, Jack, ed. **Read-Aloud Rhymes for the Very Young**. Alfred A. Knopf, 1986.
> "Hamsters" by Marci Ridlon, p. 54.
> "Cats and Dogs" by Marci Ridlon, p. 54.
> "Mice" by Rose Fyleman, p. 24.

Sing a Song of Popcorn. Scholastic, 1988.
> "Good Morning" by Muriel Sipe, p. 62.
> "To a Squirrel at Kyle-Na-No" by William Butler Yeats, p. 72.

MARCH

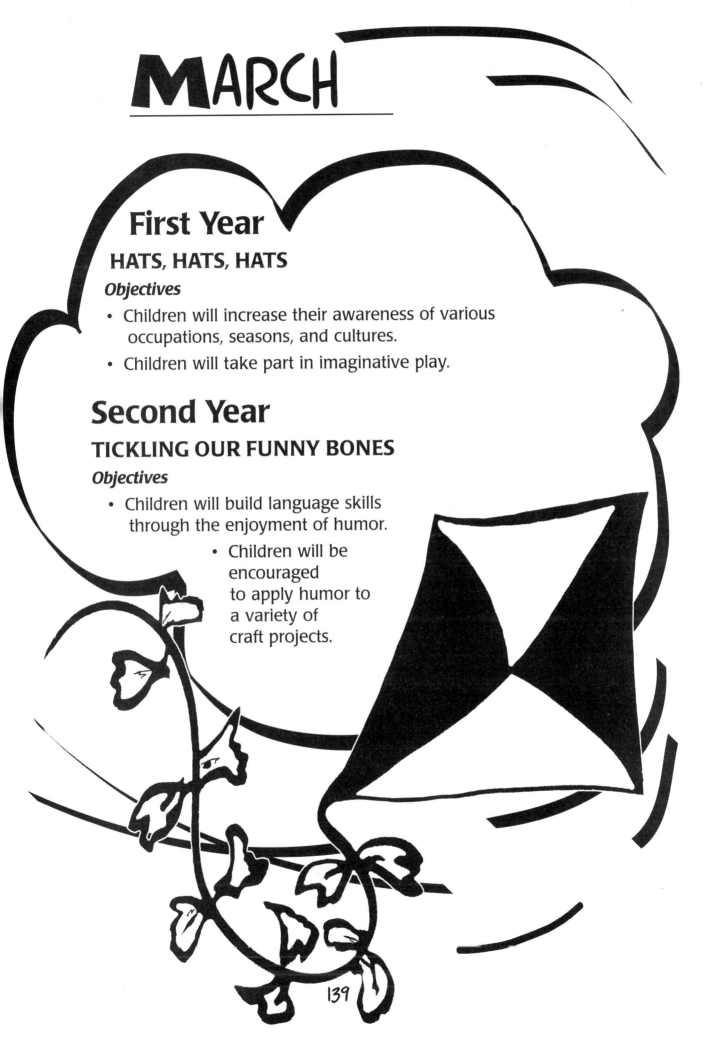

First Year

HATS, HATS, HATS

Objectives

- Children will increase their awareness of various occupations, seasons, and cultures.
- Children will take part in imaginative play.

Second Year

TICKLING OUR FUNNY BONES

Objectives

- Children will build language skills through the enjoyment of humor.
- Children will be encouraged to apply humor to a variety of craft projects.

COMMENTARY

March Topics

Hats, Hats, Hats is a fun topic for the Sharing Circle. Many children adore hats and use them for pretend play. Sharing a hat at circle time can be a vehicle for many kinds of discussion and role-play. Children brainstorm reasons why people wear various types of hats. If hats from other countries or cultures are introduced, children may make comparisons with their own hats. Children may also see hats worn by different kinds of workers or athletes.

Children readily respond to the theme, **Tickling Our Funny Bones**. Already at three years of age, children have senses of humor and start to experiment with silly language. They love nonsense words and laugh at simple incongruities. At three-and-a-half, children enjoy making merry with other children. They often act wild and silly. Nonsense rhyming is a popular activity. Four-year-olds especially have fun with language. They are at the age when they try out new words and play with them. They adore silly language and often enjoy having familiar stories or songs sung in silly ways.

Five-year-olds like to say ridiculous things, although they do not engage in as much silly language as they once did. They enjoy slapstick humor—minor disasters or misfortunes tickle their funny bones. At six, children engage in much silly giggling and often show off to call attention to themselves. When children are seven, they are amused by riddles and enjoy the kind of humor found in the *Amelia Bedelia* books.

Children particularly enjoy bringing things to the Sharing Circle that "tickle their funny bones." This use of word play and rhyme develops language skills and laughing together strengthens group cohesiveness. When choosing books to read to children this month, it is important to know the developmental stage of the children's humor.

Reference

Hamilton et. al. *Resources for Creative Teaching in Early Childhood Education*. Harcourt Brace Jovanovich, 1990. Includes good directions for making many different kinds of hats.

HATS, HATS, HATS
LETTER TO PARENTS

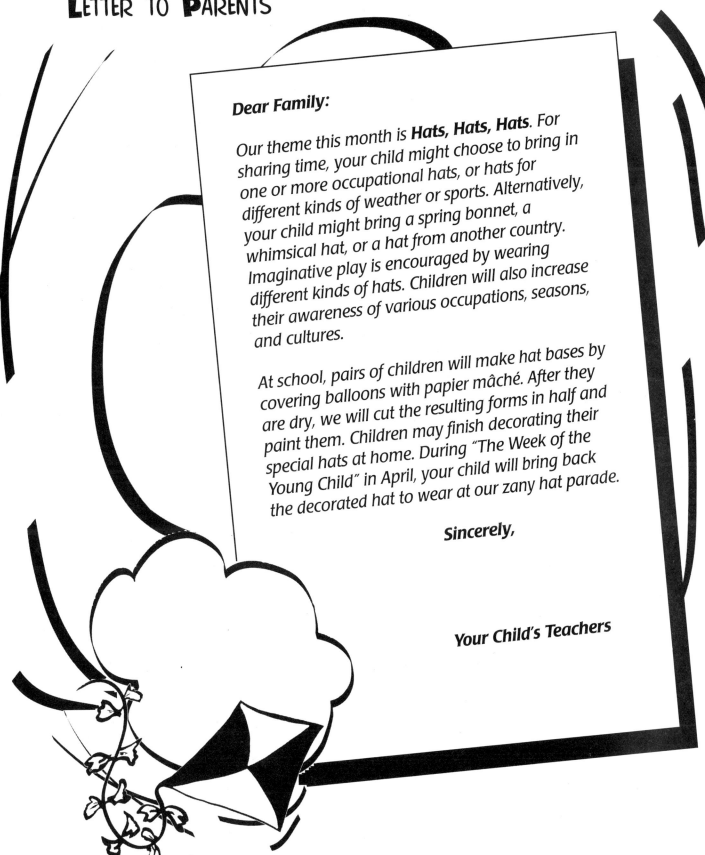

Dear Family:

Our theme this month is **Hats, Hats, Hats**. For sharing time, your child might choose to bring in one or more occupational hats, or hats for different kinds of weather or sports. Alternatively, your child might bring a spring bonnet, a whimsical hat, or a hat from another country. Imaginative play is encouraged by wearing different kinds of hats. Children will also increase their awareness of various occupations, seasons, and cultures.

At school, pairs of children will make hat bases by covering balloons with papier mâché. After they are dry, we will cut the resulting forms in half and paint them. Children may finish decorating their special hats at home. During "The Week of the Young Child" in April, your child will bring back the decorated hat to wear at our zany hat parade.

Sincerely,

Your Child's Teachers

TICKLING OUR FUNNY BONES
LETTER TO PARENTS

Dear Family:

Through our monthly theme, **Tickling Our Funny Bones**, we hope to share laughter and merriment as well as build language skills through the enjoyment of humor. For sharing time, your child might tell a joke, share a nonsensical poem or amusing story, show a humorous picture, sing a silly song, or bring a comical toy. On St. Patrick's Day, we will read limericks. As a culminating activity to our month of fun, we will celebrate April Fools' Day by having a "Silly Parade." This will occur in April during "The Week of the Young Child." Your child may wear something silly or wear clothing backwards. We will need some parent volunteers to help paint children's faces or knees for our parade.

Sincerely,

Your Child's Teachers

142

SUGGESTED ACTIVITIES FOR MARCH

COOKING PROJECTS

Green Vegetables

Have children bring a plastic zipper bag of cut green vegetables to celebrate St. Patrick's Day. Children may observe the different shades of green. Challenge them to arrange the zipper bags of veggies in order from lightest to darkest green. Make Spinach-Yogurt Dip (see page 70) to have with the cut-up green veggies.

Irish Soda Bread

Read *Bread, Bread, Bread* by Ann Morris and talk about bread from around the world. Children may practice measuring and mixing ingredients as they make Irish Soda Bread for St. Patrick's Day. You may wish to invite some parents to help with the breadmaking.

Irish Soda Bread

2 1/2 cups whole
   wheat flour
1 1/2 Tbsp. sugar
2 1/2 tsp. baking soda
1 tsp. salt

2 Tbsp. butter
1 cup raisins
2 Tbsp. caraway seeds
1 1/2 cups buttermilk
2 eggs, lightly beaten

In a large bowl, combine 2 cups of white flour, the whole wheat flour, sugar, baking soda, and salt. Add butter and work in with a pastry blender until well mixed. Stir in raisins and caraway seeds.

In a small bowl, combine buttermilk and eggs. Stir this into the flour mixture, beating ingredients until dough forms a ball. Turn dough out onto a floured surface and work in as much of the remaining white flour as needed to make a soft but not sticky dough. Knead dough for 1 to 2 minutes or until smooth.

Shape dough into a fat 8-inch (20 cm) pancake. Place on greased baking sheet. Using a floured knife, cut an "X" 1/4 inch (6.25 mm) deep across top.

Bake in preheated 350° oven 45 to 55 minutes.

ARTS & CRAFTS PROJECTS

Paper Bag Kites

Help children open up the bottom of pastel-colored lunch bags to allow air to flow through. Invite children to decorate their paper bag kites with crayons or markers. One end of the paper bag should be folded over for strength. A yarn handle may be affixed by attaching yarn to each corner of the bag and then bringing the four strands together in a knot. Attach strong string to knotted yarn for children to hold.

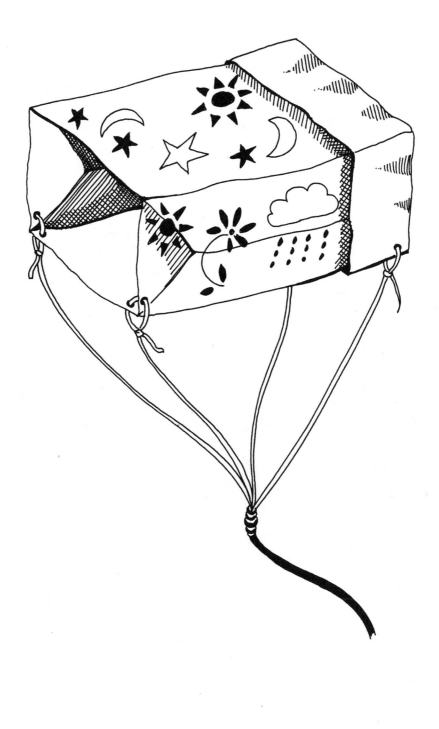

March Wind Paintings

Show children how to use straws to blow paint into designs on fingerpaint or freezer paper (so paint does not sink in too readily). Pastel tempera paints may be spooned onto the papers in two or three places for children to blow on. If appropriate for your students, invite children to work with partners. Partners stand opposite each other with the painting project between them.

Patchwork Easter Eggs

Give each child one hard-boiled egg to decorate. Cut up several small squares of brightly-colored tissue paper for each child. Show children how to brush a thin adhesive solution (methyl cellulose) onto each section of egg on which they are about to work. They will place the tissue-paper squares on the dampened egg. When the tissue is dried, it may be easily removed. The colors bleed onto the egg, leaving behind a colorful patchwork design.

ART FOR ST. PATRICK'S DAY

Green Fingerpainting

Use one of the recipes on page 235 to make green fingerpaint for children to use. Place shamrock stickers on the paintings when dry. While children are painting, you may wish to read *Clever Tom and the Leprechaun* by Linda Shute.

HATS, HATS, HATS

RELATED ARTS & CRAFTS PROJECT

Papier Mâché Hats

Use 7" (17.5 cm) round balloons of good quality as hat forms. Use strips of tagboard stapled into circles as base supports for the balloons. Help children tear newspaper into short strips. Make a soupy paste with white flour and water or use wallpaper paste. Show children how to put papier mâché on the bottoms of the balloons first to give them some weight and keep them steady. Invite children to work with partners to make a thick hat form by totally covering the balloons with papier mâché. When dry, slice hat forms in half with a utility knife. Each child takes one of the halves home to decorate for the hat parade.

TICKLING OUR FUNNY BONES

RELATED ARTS & CRAFTS PROJECTS

Silly Pickle Pictures

Read Marc Brown's *Pickle Things* to children. Give each child a green pickle shape cut from construction paper to use as a motivational starter. What can they make out of it? A pickle person? A pickle-mobile? Invite children to glue their pickles on white drawing paper and add details with crayons or markers.

Hairy Egg People

You will need enough clean, dry eggshell halves for each child to have one. Soak a package of alfalfa seeds overnight. Invite children to decorate empty eggshell halves by painting on faces with melted crayons. Place dampened cotton balls into eggshell halves and have children sprinkle the moistened alfalfa seeds on top. Within a few days, the egg people will sprout "hair."

Silly Stuff

Mix liquid starch and white glue together in equal proportions to make a putty-like mixture children will enjoy playing with. You may wish to experiment with color by adding liquid or paste food coloring to the mixture.

String Paintings

Combine equal amounts of liquid tempera and liquid starch in small bowls. Offer children a variety of colors and several lengths of string or yarn. Show children how to dip the string or yarn into the colored liquid, using a craft stick or tongue depressor to submerge the string into the paint. Children may then drag the strings across sheets of drawing paper and arrange them in interesting patterns on the paper. The string or yarn is allowed to dry on the paper (the starch acts as an adhesive).

Mud Paintings

Read *Piggy in the Puddle* by Charlotte Pomerantz to the class. Add some liquid soap and liquid starch to mud to increase its transparency and invite children to use the mixture as they would fingerpaint. This makes a terrific outdoor activity. Be sure to supply a dishpan of soapy water for hand washing.

HATS, HATS, HATS

RELATED SONG

Mexican Hat Dance   Mexican Folk Song

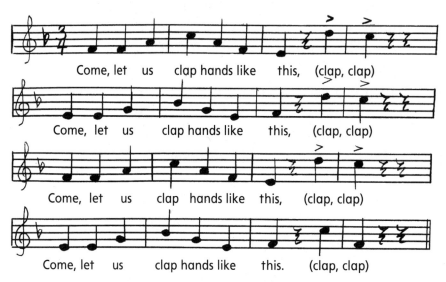

Come, let us clap hands like this, (clap, clap)

Come, let us clap hands like this, (clap, clap)

Come, let us clap hands like this, (clap, clap)

Come, let us clap hands like this. (clap, clap)

2. Come, let us stamp feet like this. *(stamp, stamp)*

Children make a circle around a Mexican hat as they dance. Invite children to suggest other movements.

A tall hat,
A small hat,
A big hat,
A cap.
Now I'll take my hats off,
And put them in my lap.

St. Patrick's Day

Traditional

We're wear-ing green for the I-rish; we're wear-ing green for the
I-rish; we're wear-ing green for the I-rish on this St. Pat-rick's Day.

2. We'll dance a jig for the Irish, *(repeat three times)*
   On this St. Patrick's Day.

3. Me fither and mither are Irish, *(repeat three times)*
   And I am Irish, too!

4. We keep a pig in the parlor, *(repeat three times)*
   And he is Irish, too!

There was a young farmer of Leeds
Who swallowed six packets of seeds.
It soon came to pass
He was covered with grass,
And he couldn't sit down for the weeds.

– Anonymous

FEATURED BOOK

Shute, Linda. ***Clever Tom and the Leprechaun: An Old Irish Story***. Lothrop, Lee & Shepard, 1988.

Clever Tom Fitzpatrick thinks his fortune is made when he captures a leprechaun and forces him to reveal the hiding place of his gold, but the leprechaun is clever too.

TICKLING OUR FUNNY BONES

RELATED SONGS

Aiken Drum

Old Scottish Folk Song

There was a man lived in the moon, lived in the moon, lived in the moon.

There was a man lived in the moon and his name was Ai-ken Drum.

2. And he played upon a ladle, a ladle, a ladle,
    And he played upon a ladle,
    And his name was Aiken Drum.

3. And his hat was made of cream cheese, cream cheese, cream cheese,
    And his hat was made of cream cheese,
    And his name was Aiken Drum.

4. And his coat was made of roast beef, roast beef, roast beef,
    And his coat was made of roast beef,
    And his name was Aiken Drum.

Children may enjoy substituting some of their favorite foods. What were his pants, shoes, and shirt made of? Invite children to draw pictures of Aiken Drum.

Wouldn't it be funny —
Wouldn't it now —
If the dog said, "Moo-oo"
And the cat sang and whistled,
And the bird said, "Mia-ow"
Wouldn't it be funny,
Wouldn't it now?

       — Anonymous

Hey Diddle Diddle   **Mother Goose**

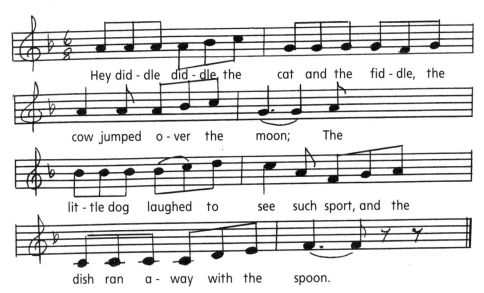

Hey did - dle did - dle, the cat and the fid - dle, the
cow jumped o - ver the moon; The
lit - tle dog laughed to see such sport, and the
dish ran a - way with the spoon.

Children enjoy miming the words to this nonsensical song.

For the following rhyming game, tell children you will tell them a little story. At each pause, they are to say, "Just like me."

"I went up one pair of stairs."
"Just like me."

"I went up two pairs of stairs."
"Just like me."

"I went into a room."
"Just like me."

"And there I saw a monkey."
"Just like me."

　　　　　　　– Anonymous

HATS, HATS, HATS

RELATED PICTURE BOOKS

Asch, Frank. ***Happy Birthday, Moon***. Prentice Hall, 1982.
When a bear discovers that the moon shares his birthday,
he buys the moon a beautiful hat as a present.

Berenstain, Stan. ***Old Hat, New Hat***. Random House, 1970.
Can the perfect old hat really be replaced by a new one?

Blos, Joan. ***Martin's Hats***. Morrow, 1984.
A variety of hats afford Martin many adventures.

Clymer, Eleanor. ***Belinda's New Spring Hat***. Franklin Watts, 1969.
Belinda tries on most of the receptacles in the house while
looking for a spring hat. Then Daddy solves the problem by
giving her—a flowerpot?

Geringer, Laura. ***A Three Hat Day***. Harper & Row, 1985.
A hat collector is having a very bad day until he meets his
true love in the hat section of the department store.

Gill, Madeline. ***The Spring Hat***. Simon & Schuster, 1993.
Though Mother Bunny's children cause her to lose her hat,
they make it up to her very nicely.

Hest, Amy. ***Fancy Aunt Jess***. Morrow, 1990.
A girl enjoys being with her unmarried Aunt Jess, who lives
in Brooklyn.

Howard, Elizabeth. *Aunt Flossie's Hat*. Clarion Books, 1990.
Sara and Susan share tea, cookies, crab cakes, and stories
about hats when they visit their favorite relative, Aunt Flossie.

Morris, Ann. *Hats, Hats, Hats*. Lothrop, Lee & Shepard, 1989.
Introduces with colored photos a variety of hats, from soft
and hard hats to snuggly and hooded hats.

Nodset, Joan. *Who Took the Farmer's Hat?* HarperCollins, 1963.
The wind blows away the farmer's hat and he finds it being
used in a most surprising way.

Polacco, Patricia. *Chicken Sunday*. Philomel Books, 1992.
To thank old Eula for her wonderful Sunday chicken
dinners, the children sell decorated eggs and buy her a
beautiful Easter hat.

Scheller, Melanie. *My Grandfather's Hat*. Margaret K. McElderry
Books, 1992.
A boy recalls his special relationship with his grandfather by
playing with his grandfather's old hat.

Slobodkina, Esphyr. *Caps for Sale: A Tale of a Peddler, Some
Monkeys, and Their Monkey Business*. Harper & Row, 1985.
A band of mischievous monkeys steals every one of a
peddler's caps while he takes a nap under a tree.

TICKLING OUR FUNNY BONES

RELATED PICTURE BOOKS

Abolafia, Yorsi. *A Fish for Mrs. Gardenia*. Greenwillow Books, 1988.
A series of haphazard events threatens to spoil Mr. Bennett's dinner with Mrs. Gardenia after his fish disappears from his outside grill, but a final accident returns the fish to its rightful place.

Allen, Pamela. *Who Sank the Boat?* Coward-McCann, 1983.
The reader is invited to guess who causes the boat to sink when five animal friends of varying sizes decide to go for a row.

Allard, Harry. *The Stupids Step Out*. Houghton Mifflin, 1974.
The Stupid family and their dog Kitty have a fun-filled day doing ridiculous things.

Baker, Alan. *Benjamin's Portrait*. Lothrop, Lee & Shepard, 1987.
Benjamin the hamster tries to paint his portrait with some unexpected results.

Barrett, Judi. *Animals Should Definitely Not Act Like People*. Atheneum, 1980.
Depicts the inconveniences animals would be burdened with if they behaved like people.

Barrett, Judi. *Animals Should Definitely Not Wear Clothing*. Atheneum, 1970.
Pictures of animals wearing clothes show why this would be a ridiculous custom for them to adopt.

Boynton, Sandra. *Hippos Go Berserk*. Little, Brown, 1979.
Larger and larger groups of hippos join a lone hippopotamus for a night-time party.

Brown, Marc. *Pickle Things*. Parents' Magazine Press, 1980.
Describes in rhyme the many things a pickle isn't.

Burningham, John. ***Mr. Gumpy's Motor Car***. Crowell, 1976.
   Mr. Gumpy's human and animal friends squash into his old car and go for a drive—until it starts to rain.

Campbell, Wayne. ***What a Catastrophe!*** Bradbury Press, 1986.
   A young boy relates what happens when he brings a frog home for breakfast. The reader is invited to choose the ending.

Flanders, Michael. ***The Hippopotamus Song: A Muddy Love Story***. Little, Brown, 1991.
   Lovestruck hippos and their muddy escapades provide inspiration for a humorous song. Music included with the book.

Gammell, Stephen. ***Git Along, Old Scudder***. Lothrop, Lee & Shepard, 1983.
   Old Scudder, traveling through the West with his dog Pilgrim, can't tell where he is until he draws a map and names the places on it.

Glazer, Tom. ***On Top of Spaghetti***. Doubleday, 1982.
   A parody, sung to the tune of "On Top of Old Smokey," tracing the meanderings of a meatball that was sneezed off a plate of spaghetti.

Hutchins, Pat. ***Rosie's Walk***. Macmillan, 1968.
   Although unaware that a fox is after her as she takes a walk around the farmyard, Rosie the hen still manages to lead him into one accident after another.

Kellogg, Steven. ***There Was an Old Woman***. Parents' Magazine Press, 1974.
   A retelling of the little old lady who swallowed a fly. The traditional verse tale of the old woman with peculiar eating habits.

Lord, John. ***The Giant Jam Sandwich***. Houghton Mifflin, 1973.
   When four million wasps fly into their village, the citizens of Itching Down devise a way of getting rid of them.

Lorenz, Lee. ***Big Gus and Little Gus***. Prentice-Hall, 1982.
When two friends go out into the world to seek their
fortune, Big Gus is rewarded despite his foolishness.

Mahy, Margaret. ***17 Kings and 42 Elephants***. Dial Books, 1987.
Seventeen kings and 42 elephants romp with a variety of
jungle animals during their journey through a wet, wild night.

Martin, Bill. ***The Happy Hippopotami***. Holt, Rinehart & Winston, 1970.
Dozens of happy hippopotami have a fun-filled holiday at
the beach.

Matsuoka, Kyoko. ***There's a Hippo in My Bath!*** Doubleday, 1982.
A turtle, two penguins, and other unlikely animals join a
young boy in his bath.

McPhail, David. ***Andrew's Bath***. Little, Brown, 1984.
Andrew's first all-by-himself bath proves an adventurous
experience.

Numeroff, Laura. ***If You Give a Moose a Muffin***. HarperCollins, 1991.
Chaos can ensue if you give a moose a muffin and start
him on a cycle of urgent requests.

Numeroff, Laura. ***If You Give a Mouse a Cookie***. Harper & Row, 1985.
Relating the cycle of requests a mouse is likely to make
after you give him a cookie takes the reader through a
young child's day.

Offen, Hilda. ***A Fox Got My Socks***. Dutton, 1992.
A gust of wind blows a small child's laundry away.

Parker, Nancy. ***Love from Uncle Clyde***. Dodd, Mead, 1977.
A little boy receives a hippopotamus from his Uncle Clyde
in Africa for his birthday with instructions on how to take
care of it.

Pearson, Susan. ***Well, I Never!*** Simon & Schuster, 1990.
A topsy-turvy day on an Iowa farm results in misplaced
breakfast food, flying pigs, and farm buildings in the clouds.

Pomerantz, Charlotte. ***The Piggy in the Puddle***. Macmillan, 1974.
Unable to persuade a young pig from frolicking in the mud, her family finally joins her for a mud party.

Raskin, Ellen. ***Who, Said Sue, Said Whoo?*** Atheneum, 1973.
Cumulative verse reveals the sounds made by various animals, but who said chitter-chitter-chatter?

Seeger, Pete. ***The Foolish Frog***. Macmillan, 1973.
A folk song.

Seuss, Dr. ***McElligot's Pool***. Random House, 1947.
A boy imagines the rare and wonderful fish he might catch in McElligot's pool.

Slepian, Jan. ***The Hungry Thing***. Follett Publishing Co., 1967.
The Hungry Thing comes to town and asks for tickles and feet loaf and other interesting things to eat while the townspeople try to figure out what he means.

Slobodkina, Esphyr. ***Caps for Sale: A Tale of a Peddler, Some Monkeys and Their Monkey Business***. Harper & Row, 1985.
A band of mischievous monkeys steals every one of a peddler's caps while he takes a nap under a tree.

Stevens, Janet. ***Tops and Bottoms***. Harcourt Brace Jovanovich, 1995.
Hare turns his bad luck around by striking a clever deal with the rich and lazy bear down the road.

Thomas, Patricia. ***"Stand Back," Said the Elephant, "I'm Going to Sneeze!"*** Lothrop, Lee & Shepard, 1971.
Knowing the havoc it will cause, all the animals try to prevent the elephant from sneezing.

Watson, Pauline. ***The Walking Coat***. Walker, 1979.
The first time he wears Uncle Charley's discarded winter coat, Scott finds himself involved in several interesting situations.

Willard, Nancy. ***Simple Pictures Are Best***. Harcourt Brace Jovanovich, 1977.

> A shoemaker and his wife being photographed for their wedding anniversary keep adding items to the picture despite the photographer's admonition that "Simple pictures are best."

Wood, Audrey. ***King Bidgood's in the Bathtub***. Harcourt Brace Jovanovich, 1985.

> Despite pleas from his court, a fun-loving king refuses to get out of his bathtub to rule his kingdom.

Wood, Audrey. ***The Napping House***. Harcourt Brace Jovanovich, 1984.

> In this cumulative tale, a wakeful flea atop a number of sleeping creatures causes a commotion, with just one bite.

Wood, Audrey. ***Silly Sally***. Harcourt Brace Jovanovich, 1991.

> A rhyming story of Silly Sally, who makes many friends as she travels to town—backward and upside down.

Related Poetry

Sing a Song of Popcorn. Scholastic, 1988.

> "Nicholas Ned" by Laura E. Richards, p. 104.
> "If We Walked on Our Hands" by Beatrice Schenk de Regnier, p. 105.
> "A Funny Man" by Natalie Joan, p. 106.
> "The Folk Who Live in Backward Town" by Mary Ann Hoberman, p. 107.

APRIL

First Year

MOTHER GOOSE ON THE LOOSE

Objectives

- Children will build language skills through dramatization.
- Children will enjoy the rhythm of language through thematic rhymes.

Second Year

LITTLE THINGS

Objectives

- Children will begin to understand growth in nature and become aware of spring's newness.
- Children will expand their vocabularies by learning words that indicate smallness.
- Children will learn that smallness depends upon one's perspective.

COMMENTARY

April Topics

Mother Goose on the Loose is our first theme for April. Mother Goose is part of our literary heritage and is often a child's first introduction to the world of poetry. It is the rhythm and rhyme that matter. Rhymes become etched in children's memories because of their musical quality. The Mother Goose songs in this portion of *The Sharing Circle* are about rain, which suits April very well. What child has not grown up with "Rain Rain Go Away" or "It's Raining, It's Pouring." Many children will be able to memorize these rhymes. They will enjoy dramatizing them in front of the class and wearing appropriate costumes. Children may share their rhymes for Mother's Day at school next month.

April is also a good time for the **Little Things** theme. This theme lends itself to a discussion of how the children have grown bigger and more capable since the beginning of school. A reading of the book *Big Sarah's Little Boots* by Paulette Bourgeois can lead to a discussion about how children are outgrowing their clothes.

Children often feel very small. Other people frequently seem bigger and more capable. However, stories such as the fable of "The Lion and the Mouse" can help children appreciate their own significance. Other classics, such as *The Little Engine That Could* by Watty Piper and *Elephant in a Well* by Marie Hall Ets, reinforce the same theme.

Children may compare their own growth to spring's new growth. Invite children to go for a spring walk and look for new buds and blossoms. Perhaps you can visit a farm and see baby animals born in the spring. There are also many opportunities to talk about little seeds when children are involved in gardening activities. A classic book to read is *The Carrot Seed* by Ruth Krauss.

MOTHER GOOSE ON THE LOOSE
LETTER TO PARENTS

Dear Family:

This month we will read and enjoy everyone's perennial favorites, the rhymes of Mother Goose, as we begin the theme **Mother Goose on the Loose**. For sharing time, your child may select one or more favorite Mother Goose rhymes to recite or dramatize, using any props he or she desires. In May, we will celebrate Mother's Day with our own Mother Goose Day. At this time, mothers will be invited to come to a dramatization of all the children's Mother Goose rhymes. Throughout the month, children will build language skills as they enjoy the rhythms of the English language.

Sincerely,

Your Child's Teachers

LITTLE THINGS
LETTER TO PARENTS

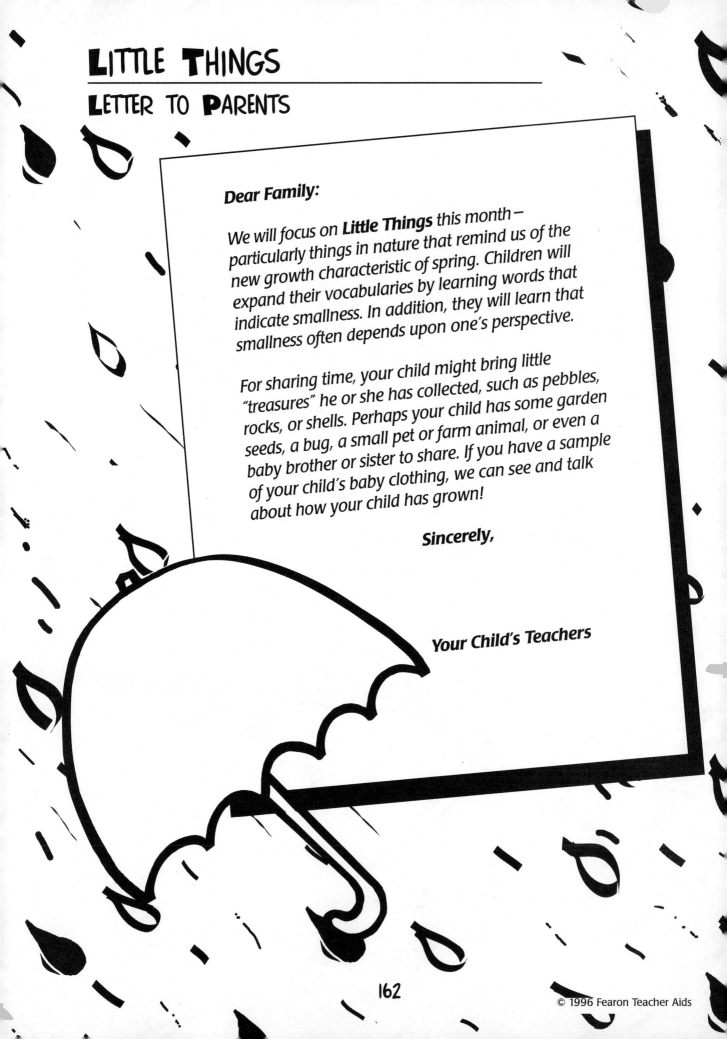

Dear Family:

We will focus on **Little Things** this month – particularly things in nature that remind us of the new growth characteristic of spring. Children will expand their vocabularies by learning words that indicate smallness. In addition, they will learn that smallness often depends upon one's perspective.

For sharing time, your child might bring little "treasures" he or she has collected, such as pebbles, rocks, or shells. Perhaps your child has some garden seeds, a bug, a small pet or farm animal, or even a baby brother or sister to share. If you have a sample of your child's baby clothing, we can see and talk about how your child has grown!

Sincerely,

Your Child's Teachers

Suggested Activities for April

Cooking Projects

Alfalfa Sprouts
Help children soak tiny alfalfa seeds and place them in screw-top mason jars. Rinse and drain the seeds over a period of several days and watch them sprout inside the jars. Children may wish to eat the sprouts sprinkled over a sandwich, such as the following.

Egg Salad Sandwiches
Give each child a hard-boiled egg in a paper cup and a plastic fork. Have children peel the eggs and chop them up. For each child, provide one teaspoon of mayonnaise and one-half teaspoon pickle relish. Children may mash in these additions and spread the mixture on slices of whole-grain bread. Add sprouts if available.

Arts & Crafts Projects

Spring Collages
Help children cut two ovals (eggs) from pastel cardstock or posterboard. Provide collage materials, such as pastel-colored buttons, white turkey feathers, pussy willows, dyed and broken-up eggshells, pastel yarns and ribbons, paper Easter grass, and pastel cotton balls, for children to arrange on their eggs. Invite them to drizzle colored glue on their collages when finished. (Glue may be colored with food coloring and placed in small squeeze bottles.)

Pussy Willow Counting
Give each child a sheet of sky blue construction paper with a long pussy willow stem drawn on the paper. Help each child roll a pair of dice, count the dots, and write the total under the pussy willow stem. Challenge children to glue an appropriate number of puffed grain cereal pieces onto each stem as pussy willow blossoms.

Rainy Day Drawings

Share Peter Spier's *Rain* with children. Sing some rain songs. Ask children: *How does it feel to be in the rain? What do you wear when you go out in the rain? Do your boots or shoes make a sound when you walk? What sound do you hear on the umbrella? Is there a special rain smell? What do the sidewalks look like? Are there any creatures that are out in the rain?* Cut out an umbrella shape for each child from colored construction paper. Give each child a sheet of blue-gray construction paper and an umbrella to glue to the paper. Invite children to use crayons to draw pictures of themselves playing outside on a rainy day.

Rain Paintings

You may wish to try the rainy day drawing project with tempera paints or markers instead of crayons. Briefly place the pictures outdoors when it is raining. Discuss with children the patterns made by the raindrops.

Rainbow Pictures

Cut a two-inch wide arch shape from 9" x 12" (22.5 cm x 30 cm) white construction paper for each child. Help children glue the arches onto sheets of sky blue paper the same size. Discuss with children the order of colors in a rainbow: red, orange, yellow, green, blue, indigo, and violet. Invite children to use pastels or watercolors to draw or paint the rainbow colors on the arches, overlapping colors slightly where they meet. Encourage them to add pictures of themselves underneath the rainbows or a pot of gold at one end.

Rainbow-Colored Paper

Invite children to fold pieces of paper towel, dip the corners of their folded towels into solutions of water and food coloring, and watch the colors spread. After dipping the towels in two or three colors, children may carefully open up their folded towels to see the designs. Use a solution of paste food colors and a bit of water for more intense colors.

ADDITIONAL IDEAS AND PROJECTS

Week of the Young Child

Invite parents and visitors to attend your celebration of the Week of the Young Child during April. First-year children may culminate the **Hats, Hats, Hats** theme with a Zany Hat Parade. Remind children to bring back to school the hats they've created from the papier mâché hat forms they made in March. They may also sing "The Mexican Hat Dance" (see page 148).

The culminating activity for **Tickling Our Funny Bones** is a Silly Parade held on April Fool's Day. Encourage children to wear their clothes backwards or in some other silly fashion. Invite parents to help paint silly faces on children's knees or paint designs on their cheeks.

Potted Marigolds

Help children plant marigold seeds in small clay pots or rinsed half-pint milk cartons (poke 2–3 holes in the bottom) at the beginning of the month. If kept in a sunny window or under grow-lights, plants will be ready for a Mother's Day presentation in May. Just before presenting the plants to their mothers (or other parents or guardians), children may add festive bows and cards to the flowerpots.

MOTHER GOOSE ON THE LOOSE

RELATED ARTS & CRAFTS PROJECTS

Hickory Dickory Dock

Discuss with children the different kinds of clocks and the sounds they make. Provide a rubber stamp clock face for children to stamp on drawing paper. Encourage them to turn the stamps into any kind of clock they wish. Invite them to draw mice in their pictures, as well as the clock hands. If you prefer, you may use Ellison clock shapes.

Old Mother Hubbard

For a motivational starter, cut "cupboard doors" into a 9" x 6" (22.5 cm x 15 cm) piece of brown construction paper for each child. Glue the "cupboards" onto white drawing paper so that children may open the doors to show the bare cupboard. Invite children to draw Old Mother Hubbard and her poor dog gazing into the empty cupboard.

Humpty Dumpty

Give children white ovals (Ellison shapes work well) on which to draw Humpty Dumpty's face. Show children how to make a crayon rubbing of an embossed tile or piece of screen on a sheet of drawing paper for Humpty Dumpty's wall. Children may glue Humpty Dumpty atop his wall. Accordion-spring arms and legs are easy additions for children to make.

Little Nanny Etticoat

For a motivational starter, make a slit in a piece of colored construction paper for each child. Slide in a strip of white cardstock as a candle that may be pulled short. Invite children to draw details to illustrate the rhyme.

Little Nanny Etticoat
In a white petticoat,
and a red nose;
The longer she stands
The shorter she grows.

Jack Be Nimble

Glue a candlestick cut from yellow construction paper onto another sheet of drawing paper as a motivational starter for each child. Glue birthday candles on the papers in the appropriate spot. Add arch-shaped slits over the candles. Invite children to draw themselves on small pieces of cardstock or index cards and attach craft-stick handles. Show children how to pass the handles through the slits to the back of the scenes to make themselves jump over the candlesticks.

There Was an Old Woman Who Lived in a Shoe

Take snapshots of each child to use for this project. Make a cutout of a large, old-fashioned shoe and glue it to the center of piece of posterboard. Give each child an index card with his or her photo glued near the top and encourage children to complete the drawings of themselves. When their pictures are ready, children may cut them out and glue them in or around the shoe on the posterboard.

LITTLE THINGS

RELATED ARTS & CRAFTS PROJECTS

Bean/Seed Collages or Mosaics

Provide an assortment of dried beans or seeds in small bowls for children to use to create collages or mosaic designs on matboard. If you choose to offer mosaics as a project, you may wish to create outlined areas for children to fill in on drawing paper, such as circles divided into eight sections or squares divided into four smaller squares or triangles. Discuss the shapes with children as they fill them in. A spray coating of high-gloss varnish adds a finished look.

"Little Things" Booklets

Create small, folded-paper journals for children. Invite them to draw their favorite little things on each page of their books or look for magazine pictures of favorite little things to glue in. Add titles and encourage children to provide illustrations for their covers.

Finger Puppets

Simple finger puppets may be made from small drawings glued to paper finger rings sized to fit each child. It is also possible to make finger puppets using old discarded cotton glove fingers. Cut index cards into one-inch strips for children to draw small characters on. Hot glue pictures to the cotton glove fingers. Encourage children to create dialogues with their finger puppets.

Ladybug Dot Designs

Read *The Grouchy Ladybug* by Eric Carle. Give each child a red circle (ladybug) and a number of stick-on dots to arrange in any way they wish. You may wish to have children roll a pair of dice and add up the dots to determine how many dots will appear on their ladybugs. Show children how to add the ladybug's head with black marker or crayon.

"Look How I've Grown!" Books

Create 4- or 5-page accordion books from 6" x 18" (15 cm x 45 cm) strips of white construction paper for each child. Invite children to draw pictures of themselves as babies on the first page and pictures of how they look now on the last page. The drawings in-between will show children getting older. Encourage children to dictate their new accomplishments to add to each page.

RELATED SONG

Rain on the Green Grass

Traditional

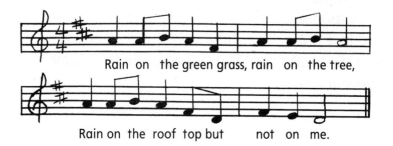

Rain on the green grass, rain on the tree,

Rain on the roof top but not on me.

The rain is raining all around,
It falls on field and tree,
It rains on the umbrellas here,
And on the ships at sea.

      – Robert Louis Stevenson

The rain was like a little mouse,
Quiet, small and gray.
It pattered all around the house
And then it went away.

      – Elizabeth Coatsworth

FEATURED BOOK

Bright, Robert. *My Red Umbrella*.
Morrow, 1959.

A young girl's umbrella grows to
accommodate an increasing
number of animal friends.

It's Raining, It's Pouring

Mother Goose

It's rain - ing, it's pour - ing, The old man is snor - ing. He went to bed and he bumped his head, and he could - n't get up in the morn- ing.

Rain, Rain, Go Away

Traditional

Rain, rain, go a - way. Come a - gain a - noth - er day. Lit - tle John - ny wants to play. Rain, rain, go a - way.

Any child's name may be substituted for "Johnny." Invite children to make rain sounds by using various body percussions, such as tapping fingers, clapping softly, or clicking the tongue.

Doctor Foster went to Gloucester
In a shower of rain;
He stepped in a puddle,
Right up to his middle,
And never went there again.

Mary Had a Little Lamb
Mother Goose

Mar-y had a lit-tle lamb, lit-tle lamb, lit-tle lamb;

Mar-y had a lit-tle lamb; it's fleece was white as snow.

2. It followed her to school one day . . .
   Which was against the rule.

3. It made the children laugh and play . . .
   To see a lamb at school.

4. And so the teacher turned it out . . .
   But still it lingered near.

5. And waited patiently about . . .
   'Til Mary did appear.

6. "Why does the lamb love Mary so . . . ?"
   The eager children cry.

7. "Why, Mary loves the lamb, you know . . ."
   The teacher did reply.

Hot Cross Buns
Mother Goose

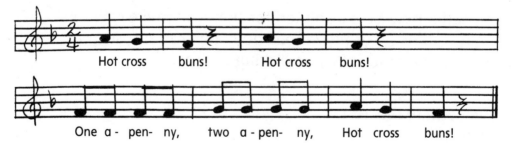

Hot cross buns! Hot cross buns!

One a-pen-ny, two a-pen-ny, Hot cross buns!

Game

Invite children to sit facing a partner. On "hot," children slap their own legs; on "cross," they clap their hands together; on "buns," the pairs of children clap each others hands. On "one a-penny," children slap their own legs. On "two a-penny," children clap their own hands.

RELATED SONGS

The Eency, Weency Spider
Traditional

The een-cy, ween-cy spi-der went up the wa-ter spout.

Down came the rain and washed the spi-der out.

Out came the sun and dried up all the rain; and the

een-cy ween-cy spi-der went up the spout a-gain.

Actions

The eency weency spider went up the water spout.
(Put tips of fingers together and pretend to make them climb spout.)

Down came the rain
(Wiggle fingers while arms come down.)

And washed the spider out.
(Sweep arms out to sides.)

Out came the sun and dried up all the rain
(Make a big circle with arms over head.)

And the eency weency spider went up the spout again.
(Fingers climb spout again.)

FEATURED BOOK

Carle, Eric. ***The Very Busy Spider***. Philomel Books, 1985.

The farm animals try to divert a busy little spider from spinning her web, but she persists and produces a thing of both beauty and usefulness. Pictures may be felt as well as seen.

LITTLE THINGS
RELATED SONGS

Six Little Ducks

Folk Song from Maryland

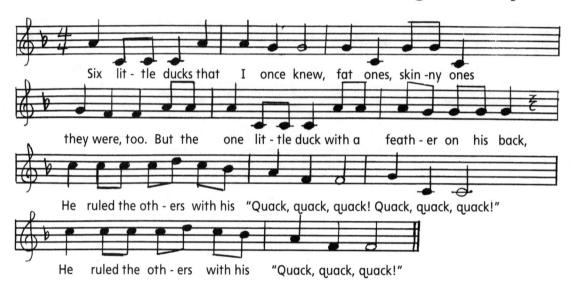

Six lit - tle ducks that I once knew, fat ones, skin -ny ones they were, too. But the one lit - tle duck with a feath - er on his back,

He ruled the oth - ers with his "Quack, quack, quack! Quack, quack, quack!"

He ruled the oth - ers with his "Quack, quack, quack!"

2. Down to the water they would go,
   Wibble wobble, wibble wobble, to and fro.
   But the one little duck with the feather on his back,
   He ruled the others with his "Quack, quack, quack!
     Quack, quack, quack!"
   He ruled the others with his "Quack, quack, quack!"

3. Home from the water they would come *(very slowly)*
   Wibble wobble, wibble wobble, ho, ho, hum!
   But the one little duck with a feather on his back *(faster)*
   He ruled the others with his "Quack, quack, quack!
     Quack, quack, quack!"
   He ruled the others with his "Quack, quack, quack!"

LITTLE THINGS

RELATED SONGS

Over in the Meadow
South Appalachian Folk Song

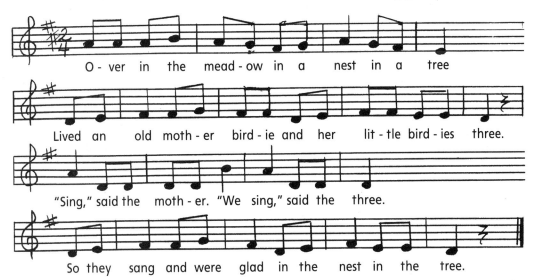

O - ver in the mead - ow in a nest in a tree

Lived an old moth - er bird - ie and her lit - tle bird - ies three.

"Sing," said the moth - er. "We sing," said the three.

So they sang and were glad in the nest in the tree.

2. Over in the meadow in the sand in the sun,
   Lived an old mother toadie and her little toadie one.
   "Hop," said the mother,
   "I hop," said the one;
   So they hopped and were glad in the sand in the sun.

Once I saw a little bird
Come hop, hop, hop
And I cried, Little Bird
Will you stop, stop, stop?

I was going to the window
To say, How do you do?
But he shook his little tail
And away he flew.

— Anonymous

RELATED SONGS

I Know a Little Pussy

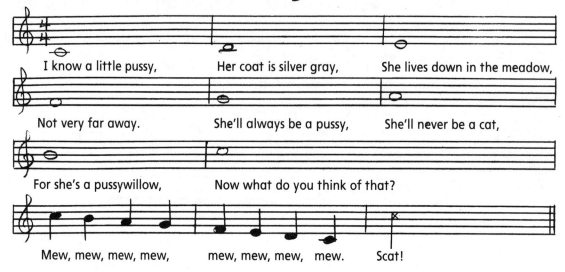

> I know a little pussy,   Her coat is silver gray,   She lives down in the meadow,
>
> Not very far away.   She'll always be a pussy,   She'll never be a cat,
>
> For she's a pussywillow,   Now what do you think of that?
>
> Mew, mew, mew, mew,   mew, mew, mew, mew.   Scat!

Action

Children begin singing the song in a crouching position. They raise themselves up a little as the notes climb the scale, until by the end, they are standing. They begin the "mews" in a standing position and bend lower with each mew. At "scat," children all jump up high.

Little Green Frog   **Traditional**

> "Gung, gung," went the lit-tle green frog one day. "Gung,
>
> gung," went the lit-tle green frog. "Gung
>
> gung," went the lit-tle green frog one day; and his
>
> eyes went "Aah, aah, gung." (put fingers around eyes; stick out tongue)

SPRING

RELATED PICTURE BOOKS

Brown, Craig. *In the Spring*. Greenwillow Books, 1994.
Spring signals the arrival of many babies, both animal and human, on the farm.

Clifton, Lucille. *The Boy Who Didn't Believe in Spring*. Dutton, 1973.
Two skeptical city boys set out to find spring which they've heard is "just around the corner."

Dabcovich, Lydia. *Sleepy Bear*. E. P. Dutton, 1982.
Shows Bear getting ready for his long winter nap, or hibernation, and his springtime awakening.

Fleischman, Susan. *The Boy Who Looked for Spring*. Harcourt Brace Jovanovich, 1993.
Ben attempts to solve three riddles about spring in order to break the spell imprisoning Mother Earth in unending sleep.

Good, Elaine. *That's What Happens When It's Spring*. Good Books. 1987.
A rural child discovers the sights, sounds, colors, and special feeling of spring.

Hines, Anna. *Come to the Meadow*. Clarion Books, 1984.
A little girl is eager to share the delights of the meadow with her family, but everyone is too busy until Granny suggests a picnic.

Hurd, Edith. *The Day the Sun Danced*. Harper & Row, 1965.
Poetic verse leads the bear, the fox, and the deer through the bleakness of winter to a final burst of color, warmth and spring.

Johnson, Crockett. ***Will Spring Be Early or Will Spring Be Late?*** Crowell, 1959.
> So anxious is the groundhog to predict an early spring that he is grossly misled by an artificial flower.

Keats, Ezra Jack. ***Over in the Meadow***. Four Winds Press, 1971.
> Verses describing the activities of various animals also illustrate the numbers one through ten.

Rockwell, Anne. ***My Spring Robin***. Macmillan, 1989.
> Before finding the robin she is searching for, a child discovers other interesting fauna and flora in her backyard.

Tafuri, Nancy. ***Rabbit's Morning***. Greenwillow Books, 1985.
> When the sun comes up a baby rabbit goes exploring in the meadow and sees many other animals.

Wood, Joyce. ***Grandmother Lucy in Her Garden***. Collins-World, 1975.
> On the first day of spring a little girl walks in the garden with her grandmother.

Ziefert, Harriet. ***Sarah's Questions***. Lothrop, Lee & Shepard, 1986.
> A little girl asks many questions about the world while taking a walk with her mother.

Zolotow, Charlotte. ***One Step, Two. . . .*** Lothrop, Lee & Shepard, 1981.
> While out for a walk on a spring morning, a little girl shows her mother things grown-ups sometimes miss.

Rain and Rainbows

Related Picture Books

Asch, Frank. **Skyfire**. Prentice-Hall, 1984.
  When he sees a rainbow for the first time, Bear thinks that the sky is on fire and he is determined to put out the skyfire.

Bright, Robert. **My Red Umbrella**. Morrow, 1959.
  A young girl's umbrella grows to accommodate an increasing number of animal friends.

Carlstrom, Nancy. **What Does the Rain Play?** Macmillan, 1993.
  A boy enjoys the various noises the rain makes.

Foster, Joanna. **Pete's Puddle**. Harcourt Brace & World, 1969.
  Pete delights in puddles and finds a perfect one in the backyard where he can make mud pies, sail boats, fill bottles, and see the world upside down.

Freeman, Don. **A Rainbow of My Own**. Viking Press, 1966.
  A small boy imagines what it would be like to have his own rainbow to play with.

Hughes, Shirley. **Alfie's Feet**. Lothrop, Lee & Shepard, 1982.
  Alfie is proud of being able to put his lovely new boots on by himself but wonders why they feel funny.

Scheffler, Ursel. **A Walk in the Rain**. Putnam's, 1986.
  Jamie goes for a walk in the rain with his grandmother and wears his new rainwear.

Serfozo, Mary. **Rain Talk**. Margaret K. McElderry Books, 1990.
  A child enjoys a glorious day in the rain, listening to the varied sounds it makes as it comes down.

Skofield, James. **All Wet, All Wet!** Harper & Row, 1984.
A small boy experiences, along with the animals of
meadow and forest, the sights, smells and sounds of a rainy
summer day.

Spier, Peter. **Peter Spier's Rain**. Doubleday, 1982.
Two children play in their backyard during a rainy day.

Vincent, Gabrielle. **Ernest and Celestine's Picnic**. Greenwillow Books,
1982.
Rain does not stop Ernest and Celestine from picnicking.

Yashima, Taro. **Umbrella**. Puffin Books, 1977.
Momo eagerly waits for a rainy day so she can use the red
boots and umbrella she received on her third birthday.

Zolotow, Charlotte. **The Storm Book**. Harper & Row, 1989.
A little boy and others watch a thunderstorm with its rain,
lightning, wind, and rainbow.

RELATED POETRY

Prelutsky, Jack, ed. **Read-Aloud Rhymes for the Very Young**. Alfred A.
Knopf, 1986.
"Ode to Spring" by Walter R. Brooks, p. 56.
"The Spring Wind" by Charlotte Zolotow, p. 56.
"Pussy Willows" by Aileen Fisher, p. 57.
"Raindrops" by Aileen Fisher, p. 60.
"Squirrel in the Rain" by Frances Frost, p. 60.
"Umbrellas" by Barbara Juster Esbensen, p. 60.
"April" by Lucille Clifton, p. 60.
"Showers" by Marchette Chute, p. 12.
"Rain on the Green Grass" by Marchette Chute, p. 12.
"Rainy Day" by William Wise, p. 13.
"Mud" by Polly Chase Boyden, p. 13.
"Sun After Rain" by Norma Farber, p. 13.

Hughes, Langston. "April Rain Song." **Sing a Song of Popcorn**.
Scholastic, 1988, p. 20.

Milne, A. A. "Happiness." **When We Were Very Young**. Dutton, 1924.

MOTHER GOOSE ON THE LOOSE

RELATED PICTURE BOOKS

Aylesworth, Jim. ***The Completed Hickory Dickory Dock***. Atheneum, 1990.

Barratt, Carol. ***The Mother Goose Songbook***. Derrydale Books, 1984.

Bayley, Nicola. ***Nicola Bailey's Book of Nursery Rhymes***. Alfred A. Knopf, 1975.

Blegvad, Lenore. ***Mittens for Kittens and Other Rhymes about Cats***. Atheneum, 1974.

Blegvad, Eric and Lenore. ***The Parrot in the Garret and Other Rhymes about Dwellings***. Atheneum, 1982.

Blegvad, Lenore. ***This Little Pig-a-Wig and Other Rhymes about Pigs***. Atheneum, 1978.

Conover, Chris. ***The Adventures of Simple Simon***. Farrar, Straus & Giroux, 1987.

Emberley, Ed. ***London Bridge Is Falling Down***. Little, Brown, 1967.

Hague, Michael. ***Mother Goose: A Collection of Classic Nursery Rhymes***. Holt, Rinehart & Winston, 1984.

Hale, Sarah. ***Mary Had a Little Lamb***. Scholastic, 1990.

Jeffers, Susan. ***If Wishes Were Horses and Other Rhymes***. Dutton, 1979.

Jeffers, Susan. ***Three Jovial Huntsmen: A Mother Goose Rhyme***. Bradbury Press, 1973.

Larrick, Nancy. ***Songs from Mother Goose with the Traditional Melody for Each***. Harper & Row, 1989.

Lucas, Barbara. ***Cats by Mother Goose***. Lothrop, Lee & Shepard, 1986.

Marshall, James. **Old Mother Hubbard and Her Wonderful Dog**. Farrar, Straus & Giroux, 1991.

Obligado, Lilian. **Three Little Kittens**. Random House, 1974.

Oxenbury, Helen. **Cakes and Custard: Children's Rhymes**. Morrow, 1975.

Oxenbury, Helen. **The Helen Oxenbury Nursery Rhyme Book**. Morrow, 1986.

Pearson, Tracey. **Sing a Song of Sixpence**. Dial Books, 1985.

Peppé, Rodney. **Simple Simon**. Holt, Rinehart & Winston, 1972.

Spier, Peter. **And So My Garden Grows**. Doubleday, 1969.

Spier, Peter. **Hurrah, We're Outward Bound**. Doubleday, 1967.

Spier, Peter. **To Market! To Market!** Doubleday, 1969.

Stevens, Janet. **The House that Jack Built: A Mother Goose Rhyme**. Holiday House, 1985.

Tripp, Wallace. **Granfa' Grig Had a Pig, and Other Rhymes without Reason**. Little, Brown, 1976.

Winter, Jeanette. **Come Out to Play**. Knopf, 1986.

LITTLE THINGS

RELATED PICTURE BOOKS

Bornstein, Ruth. *Little Gorilla*. Seabury Press, 1976.
Little Gorilla's family and friends try to help him overcome his special growing pains.

Bridwell, Norman. *A Tiny Family*. Scholastic, 1968.
When tiny people look for grandfather's umbrella they meet giant people.

Brown, Margaret Wise. *Baby Animals*. Random House, 1989.
Relates the morning, noon, and evening activities of several young animals and a little girl.

Brown, Margaret Wise. *Little Fur Family*. HarperCollins, 1946.
The experiences of the little fur child as he investigates some other creatures of the wild wood.

Carle, Eric. *The Tiny Seed*. Picture Book Studio, 1987.
A simple description of a flowering plant's life cycle through the season.

Carle, Eric. *The Very Busy Spider*. Philomel Books, 1985.
The farm animals try to divert a busy little spider from spinning her web, but she persists and produces a thing of both beauty and usefulness. The pictures may be felt as well as seen.

Cristini, Ermanno and Luigi Puricelli. *In My Garden*. Scholastic, 1981.
By close observation, little creatures can be found in the garden.

Dunn, Judy. *The Little Duck*. Random House, 1976.
Easy to read text and photographs follow the growth of a duck from incubation to adulthood.

Ets, Marie Hall. *Elephant in a Well*. Viking Press, 1972.
The combined efforts of several animals cannot pull an elephant from a well until a mouse adds his strength.

Finzel, Julia. *Large as Life*. Lothrop, Lee & Shepard, 1991.
Flying off on the back of a butterfly? Dropping in on an owl? Hiding in the coils of a snake? Spotting this ladybug isn't always easy as she flits from frog to flamingo, from peacock to whale, but young children feel enormously pleased when they find her.

Fowler, Richard. *Ladybug on the Move*. Harcourt Brace Jovanovich, 1993.
Ladybug searches for a new home, but every place she finds is already occupied. Features a separate ladybug who weaves her way through die-cut pages.

Green, Norma. *The Hole in the Dike*. Crowell, 1975.
Retells the story of the little boy whose resourcefulness and courage saved his country from being destroyed by the ocean.

Hutchins, Pat. *Titch*. Macmillan, 1971.
Nothing Titch owned amounted to much except the smallest thing of all—a seed.

Joyce, William. *George Shrinks*. Harper & Row, 1985.
Taking care of a cat and a baby brother turns into a series of comic adventures when George wakes up to find himself shrunk to the size of a mouse.

Keats, Ezra Jack. *Over in the Meadow*. Four Winds Press, 1971.
Verses describing the activities of various animals also illustrate the numbers one through ten.

Krauss, Ruth. *Big and Little*. Scholastic, 1987.
Brief text and illustrations describe some of the little things that big things love.

LaFontaine, Jean de. ***The Lion and the Rat: A Fable***. Watts, 1963.
 A retelling of the LaFontaine fable in which a small rat is the
 only animal capable of saving the life of the king of beasts.

Lionni, Leo. ***The Biggest House in the World***. Pantheon Books, 1968.
 A snail's father advises him to keep his house small and
 tells him what happened to a snail that grew a large and
 spectacular shell.

Lionni, Leo. ***Swimmy***. Random House, 1963.
 A little black fish in a school of red fish figures out a way of
 protecting them all from their natural enemies.

Mosel, Arlene. ***The Funny Little Woman***. Dutton, 1972.
 While chasing a dumpling a little lady is captured by wicked
 creatures from whom she escapes with the means of
 becoming the richest woman in Japan.

Parker, Nancy and Joan Wright. ***Bugs***. Greenwillow Books, 1989.
 Includes general information, jokes, and brief descriptions
 of the physical characteristics, habits, and natural
 environment of a variety of common insects.

Piper, Watty. ***The Little Engine That Could***. Platt & Munk, 1961.
 When the other engines refuse, the Little Blue Engine tries
 to pull a stranded train full of dolls, toys, and good food
 over the mountain.

Ryder, Joanne. ***The Snail's Spell***. Puffin Books, 1988.
 The reader imagines how it feels to be a snail.

Ryder, Joanne. ***Where Butterflies Grow***. Lodestar Books, 1989.
 Describes what it feels like to change from a caterpillar into
 a butterfly. Includes gardening tips to attract butterflies.

Schilling, Betty. ***Two Kittens Are Born: From Birth to Two Months***.
Holt, Rinehart & Winston, 1980.
 Follows the growth of two kittens from birth to two months.

Selsam, Millicent. *How Kittens Grow*. Four Winds Press, 1973.
A photographic essay describing four kittens' first eight weeks of life.

Selsam, Millicent. *How Puppies Grow*. Four Winds Press, 1971.
Describes the first six weeks of six puppies' lives as they nurse, sleep, learn to walk, eat solid food, and interact with other dogs.

Soya, Kiyoshi. *A House of Leaves*. Philomel Books, 1987.
Sheltering from the rain, Sarah shares a house of leaves with a praying mantis, ladybug, and other small creatures of the wild.

Yabuchi, Masayuki. *Whose Baby?* Philomel Books, 1985.
Introduces several animal infants and their parents.

RELATED POETRY

Prelutsky, Jack, ed. *Read-Aloud Rhymes for the Very Young*. Alfred A. Knopf, 1986.
"Little Seeds" by Else Holmelund Minarik, p. 14.
"A Spike of Green" by Barbara Baker, p. 14.
"Fuzzy Wuzzy, Creepy Crawly" by Lillian Schulz, p. 62.
"Ants" by Mary Ann Hoberman, p. 62.
"Only My Opinion" by Monica Shannon, p. 62.
"Ants Live Here" by Lilian Moore, p. 62.
"Grasshopper Green" by Nancy Dingman Watson, p. 63.
"Dragonfly" by Florence Page Jacques, p. 63.
"But I Wonder. . ." by Aileen Fisher, p. 63.

Heide, Florence Parry. "Rocks." *Sing a Song of Popcorn*. Scholastic, 1988, p. 132.

MAY

First Year

THE EARTH IS OUR MOTHER

Objectives

- A love and respect for nature will be fostered in children.
- Children will learn that they individually can have an impact on the environment.
- Children will learn about Native American harmony with nature through books and song.

Second Year: GOING PLACES

Objectives

- Children will learn about different kinds of transportation.
- Children will learn about various vacations, such as going to a beach, going camping, visiting a small town or city.
- Children will learn to tell stories in sequence.

COMMENTARY

Creating a Reverence for the Earth

If we are to sustain this planet for future generations, we must teach children to feel reverence for the earth. Children have an innate sense of curiosity and wonder. Throughout the year, teachers can marvel with children at nature's beauty. An important book to read is Rachel Carson's *The Sense of Wonder*, in which the author shares with her grandnephew her own sense of wonder and joy regarding the ocean. To heighten children's perceptual awareness, *The Sharing Circle* includes a guide for exploring fruit through the five senses (see page 228).

Children may learn to feel more a part of their surroundings by hearing stories about Native Americans. Children respond eagerly to Native American legends that describe a relationship with the earth. Children will enjoy singing and dancing to "The Earth Is Our Mother." *Brother Eagle, Sister Sky: A Message from Chief Seattle* by Susan Jeffers fosters respect and love for the Earth.

THE EARTH IS OUR MOTHER
LETTER TO PARENTS

Dear Family:

Our theme for the month is **The Earth Is Our Mother**. We think of the earth as a "mother" that nurtures and provides for us. However, we must also take good care of her in return. For sharing time, your child may bring a natural specimen, a craft your child has made using recycled materials or materials found in nature, or a poster illustrating a way to save our natural resources.

We will read books about Native Americans and their harmonious relationships with Mother Earth. A love for nature will be fostered in the children. We hope to help them become more ecologically aware and respectful of nature as well.

Sincerely,

Your Child's Teachers

189

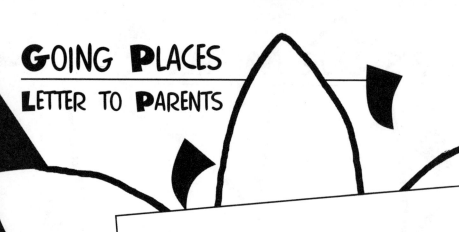

Dear Family:

Our theme for this month is **Going Places**. For sharing time, we invite your child to share pictures, maps, and souvenirs from a remembered vacation. Alternatively, your child might tell about summer vacation plans. You may wish to help your child create a photo-essay book of an actual or imagined family trip. Your child might use photographs, drawings, postcards, and mementos to tell the story. Feel free to write down your child's story in his or her own words. We may ask children questions such as, Where would you go if you could go anywhere you want for a vacation? Who would you take with you? How would you get there? What would you bring back?

Children will learn about different kinds of transportation as well as elements of geography and maps. They will consider various types of vacations, such as going to a beach, going camping, or visiting a small town or large city. The children will also practice telling stories in sequence.

Sincerely,

Your Child's Teachers

Suggested Activities for May

Cooking Projects

Banana Yogurt
Have each child bring a ripe banana to school. Encourage children to explore the outside and inside of the bananas using their five senses (see page 228). Provide plain yogurt in small bowls for each child. Invite children to mash their bananas with plastic forks and mix with the plain yogurt for a snack. Finely chopped nuts or wheat germ makes a nice topping.

Salad Bar
Plan a salad bar for the last day of school. Have children wash and tear up several varieties of lettuce in school that morning. Ask each child to bring in a plastic zipper bag of favorite salad ingredients, such as sunflower seeds, alfalfa sprouts, shredded carrots, pickled vegetables, garbanzo and kidney beans, cherry tomatoes, shredded red cabbage, croutons, raisins, slices of hard-cooked egg, scallions, sliced olives, pieces of broccoli and cauliflower. You might suggest that parents take their children to visit a supermarket salad bar to consider the possibilities. Encourage children to help prepare the ingredients at home—drain the garbanzos, cut the scallions, or whatever might be involved. Some parents may prefer to send in a bottle of dressing. Provide small bowls, forks, and napkins for the salad bar.

Arts & Crafts Projects (Mother's Day Gifts)

Candleholders
Provide an 8-inch candle and baker's clay for each child, following the recipe on page 234. Show children how to form candleholders by enclosing the bases of the candles in the clay and creating a free-standing flat base. Invite children to decorate their candleholders by embedding dried flowers and cloves in the clay. Candlesticks may air dry.

Pincushions

Give each child a six-inch (15 cm) square of muslin to decorate with pastel dye sticks or fabric crayons. Machine-sew the decorated muslin squares to backing fabric of the same size, leaving a small opening through which children may pour fine sawdust. Stitch up the openings.

Framed Photos

Photograph each child doing a favorite school activity. Show children how to "frame" their photographs using craft sticks and white glue. Encourage children to decorate their frames with markers and sequins or small beads. Cut felt backing to fit each framed photograph.

ADDITIONAL IDEAS AND PROJECTS

May Day

Fashion a Maypole out of a plumber's pipe by hanging broad ribbons from one end—one ribbon per child. Wire or hot glue an assortment of silk flowers to the top of the pole where the ribbons are hung. Plant the pole in a sturdy Christmas tree base. Invite parents and guardians to a procession and Maypole dance. Children may sing and dance to the song, "Dance in the Circle." You may also wish to play the singing game "A Tisket, A Tasket" and do a chanting activity, "The Earth Is Our Mother," to "wake up the Earth."

Mother Goose Day

This Mother's Day Celebration is a culminating activity for **Mother Goose on the Loose**. Invite mothers or guardians to join the children for a presentation of all of their Mother Goose dramatizations.

For a shared storytime, consider reading special stories about mothers, such as *Ask Mr. Bear* by Marjorie Flack and *Mr. Rabbit and the Lovely Present* by Charlotte Zolotow—changing the wording in both the stories from *birthday* to *Mother's Day*. You may wish to set up a children's book display about mothers.

Play game songs learned during the year. Friendship Fruit Salad (see page 19) would be an appropriate snack after reading *Mr. Rabbit and the Lovely Present*. Encourage children to present their hand-made gifts to their mothers or guardians.

Day at a Nature Park

Invite parents to prepare picnic lunches and accompany children on a visit to a nature park. Point out to children how the trees have changed since the fall. You may wish to play parachute games, make sun prints, and look for animal tracks in the mud. Bring along some plaster of Paris and a bucket for water. If children locate interesting animal tracks, you can slip a cardboard ring around the animal print and pour in plaster of Paris to make a mold. Prepare lists for a scavenger hunt or make simple maps of the area for children to follow (in small groups with adult guidance) to find special treasures or dessert items. Be sure to indicate geographical features such as "big maple tree" or "rock wall" on the map.

Last Day of School Picnic

Invite parents and guardians to school for a picnic lunch. Everyone brings his or her own sandwich and something to share for a salad bar (see page 191). Provide lemonade and lettuce. You may wish to have children decorate brown paper grocery bags (the kind with handles work well) in which to take home all their accumulated projects and mementos.

THE EARTH IS OUR MOTHER
RELATED ARTS & CRAFTS PROJECTS

Trash Art

Collect and invite parents to collect an assortment of small boxes, spools, lids, Styrofoam trays, bottle caps, cardboard tissue tubes, aluminum baking pans, and so on. Lumber yards and electric supply companies are good sources for materials as well. Invite children to turn these recycled items into trash-art sculptures and collages. Keep a supply of masking tape and paint to help children attach and decorate their constructions. Large appliance boxes can become any number of buildings or vehicles and make a great cooperative group project.

Class Terrarium

Have children cover the bottom of a glass aquarium or big, round fishbowl with gravel for drainage. Invite them to add planting soil and stones. Then children may carefully add some rooted cuttings from houseplants or some small ferns and arrange moss around the plants. Encourage children to decorate the terrarium with small animal figures. Show them how to use a spray bottle to keep the soil moist. You may wish to sink a small can or bowl into the soil as a pond and keep it filled with water. Cover the top of the terrarium with a piece of Plexiglas cut to size.

GOING PLACES

RELATED ARTS & CRAFTS PROJECTS

Things that Go Montage

Invite children to look through magazines for pictures of things that "go"—on the road, on the water, in the air, on snow and ice, in the city, in the country, in the park, in the yard, in the house, and so on. Have children create a montage of pictures on a large sheet of butcher paper.

Going Places Pictures

Take photographs of each child for this project. Cut out each child's face and glue it in the center of a sheet of drawing paper. Invite children to complete the drawings by placing themselves behind the wheel of any vehicle they choose, such as an airplane or a tractor. Alternatively, they might be looking out the window of a plane or train. Underneath each illustration, help children complete the sentence, (child's name) is going places!

John is going places!

RELATED SONGS

Dance in the Circle **Louisiana Folk Song**

Dance in the cir - cle, dance in the ring;

Dance in the morn - ing to wel - come the Spring.

Dance

Dance in the circle, *(walk to the right)*
Dance in the ring; *(walk to the left)*
Dance in the morning *(walk to the center)*
To welcome the Spring *(step backwards out of the circle)*

This song could be used around the Maypole.

FEATURED BOOK

Carlstrom, Nancy. ***Wild Wild Sunflower Anna***. Macmillan, 1987.

Spending a day outdoors, Anna revels in the joys of sun, sky, grass, flowers, berries, frogs, ants, and beetles.

Under the Maypole

Dan - cing un - der the May - pole hold - ing rib - bons so gay;

We shall al - ways re - mem - ber our class - mates of to - day.

A Tribute to Old Friends

Make new friends but keep the old;

One is sil - ver and the oth - er gold.

The Earth Is Our Mother

Traditional Native American

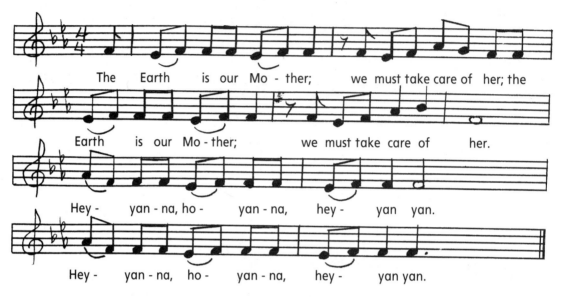

The Earth is our Mo-ther; we must take care of her; the

Earth is our Mo-ther; we must take care of her.

Hey-yan-na, ho-yan-na, hey-yan yan.

Hey-yan-na, ho-yan-na, hey-yan yan.

From *A Circle Is Cast: Rounds, Chants and Songs for Celebration and Ritual.* LIBANA. Used by permission.

Dance

Keep the beat by playing a hand drum. Invite children to stand in a circle and gently slap the sides of their legs and bend their knees slightly on each beat. When the song begins, everyone claps hands rhythmically and slowly raises their hands above their heads while moving gradually into the middle of the circle. On the repeat, everyone returns to their original places in the circle while clapping hands to the rhythm. On the refrain, everyone moves around the circle to the right for the first two measures and to the left for the final two measures.

I'm glad the sky is painted blue
And earth is painted green
With such a lot of nice fresh air
All sandwiched in between.

     – Anonymous

As my eyes
Search the prairie,
I feel the summer in the spring.

     – Chippewa

GOING PLACES

RELATED SONGS

We Go Traveling

**Words by W.S. Williams,
French Folk Song**

Go by car, go by train. Go by boat or go by plane.

2. Here we go, in a car,
   Trav'ling near and trav'ling far.

3. When we sail in a boat,
   On the water we will float.

4. We can ride in a train
   In the sun and in the rain.

5. Roller skates on our feet,
   Send us rolling down the street.

6. On our bikes we will roam,
   'Round the block and back to home.

7. We will ride in a bus,
   Come and wave good-bye to us.

8. In a plane we can fly,
   Soaring up into the sky.

From *Music Through the Day*, Silver Burdett, 1962. Used by permission.

AT THE SEASIDE
*When I was down beside the sea
A wooden spade they gave to me
To dig the sandy shore.*

*My holes were empty like a cup.
In every hole the sea came up,
'Til it could come no more.*

– Robert Louis Stevenson

THE AIRPLANE
*The airplane taxies down the field
And heads into the breeze,
It lifts its wheels above the ground,
It skims above the trees,
It rises high and higher
Away up toward the sun,
It's just a speck against the sky
–And now it's gone!*

– Unknown

Goodbye Song

Folk Song "Miss Jennie Ann Jenkins" (Adapted)

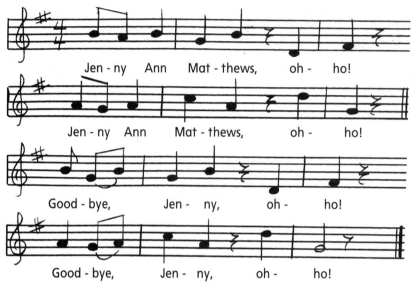

Jen - ny Ann Mat - thews, oh - ho!

Jen - ny Ann Mat - thews, oh - ho!

Good - bye, Jen - ny, oh - ho!

Good - bye, Jen - ny, oh - ho!

2. Where is my Jenny? Oh-ho!
   Where is my Jenny? Oh-ho!
   She's gone to Texas, Oh-ho!
   She's gone to Texas, Oh-ho!

Riding in a Car

South Carolina Folk Song

Rid - ing in a car, Jus - tin, Jus - tin, Jus - tin,

Rid - ing in a car, Jus - tin, I'm a long way from home.

MOTHERS

RELATED PICTURE BOOKS

Bunting, Eve. **The Mother's Day Mice**. Clarion Books, 1986.
Three little mouse brothers go into the meadow to find a
present for their mother but it is the littlest mouse that comes
up with the most unusual gift of all.

Flack, Marjorie. **Ask Mr. Bear**. Macmillan, 1958.
When he doesn't know what to give his mother for her
birthday, a small boy asks all the animals for advice.

Joosse, Barbara. **Mama, Do You Love Me?** Chronicle Books, 1991.
A child living in the Arctic learns that a mother's love is
unconditional.

Kroll, Steven. **Happy Mother's Day**. Holiday House, 1985.
One day when Mom returns home she is greeted by surprise
after surprise from each of her six children and her husband.

Mayer, Mercer. **Just for You**. Golden Press, 1975.
A little creature tries and tries to do something special for his
mother but something always seems to go wrong.

Munsch, Robert. **Love You Forever**. Firefly Books, 1986.
A mother continues to rock her son when he's asleep and
sing of her love for him as he grows, until he must rock and
sing to her in her old age.

Murphy, Jill. **Five Minutes Peace**. Putnam, 1986.
Mrs. Large tries to take a peaceful, relaxing bath but her
family has other ideas.

Polushkin, Maria. **Mother, Mother, I Want Another**. Crown Publishing,
1978.
Anxious to get her son to sleep, Mrs. Mouse goes off to find
what she thinks he wants.

Scott, Ann. **On Mother's Lap**. Clarion Books, 1992.
A small Eskimo boy discovers that Mother's lap is a very
special place with room for everyone.

Zolotow, Charlotte. **This Quiet Lady**. Greenwillow Books, 1991.
A child finds out about Mother's early life by looking at old
pictures.

THE EARTH IS OUR MOTHER

RELATED PICTURE BOOKS

Bierhorst, John. ***The Woman Who Fell from the Sky; The Iroquois Story of Creation***. Morrow, 1993.
> Describes how the creation of the world was begun by a woman who fell down to earth from the sky country, and how it was finished by her two sons, Sapling and Flint.

Cherry, Lynne. ***A River Ran Wild: An Environmental History***. Harcourt Brace Jovanovich, 1992.
> An environmental history of the Nashua River from its discovery by Indians through the polluting years of the Industrial Revolution to the ambitious cleanup that revitalized it.

Goble, Paul. ***Crow Chief: A Plains Indian Story***. Orchard Books, 1992.
> Crow Chief always warns the buffalo that hunters are coming, until Falling Star, a saviour, comes to camp, tricks Crow Chief and teaches him that all must share and live like relatives together.

Goble, Paul. ***Death of the Iron Horse***. Macmillan, 1987.
> In an act of bravery and defiance against the white men encroaching on their territory in 1867, a group of young Cheyenne braves derail and raid a freight train.

Goble, Paul. ***Dream Wolf***. Bradbury Press, 1990.
> When two Plains Indian children become lost, they are cared for and guided safely home by a friendly wolf.

Goble, Paul. ***The Girl Who Loved Wild Horses***. Macmillan, 1978.
> Though she is fond of her people, a girl prefers to live among the wild horses where she is truly happy and free.

Jeffers, Susan. ***Brother Eagle, Sister Sky: A Message from Chief Seattle***. Dial Books, 1991.
> A Squamish Indian chief describes his people's respect and love for the earth, and concern for its destruction.

Locker, Thomas. *The Land of the Gray Wolf*. Dial Books, 1991.
Running Deer and his fellow tribesmen take special care of
their land until they lose it to invading white settlers, who
wear it out and leave it to recover on its own.

Luenn, Nancy. *Mother Earth*. Atheneum, 1992.
Describes the gifts that the earth gives to us and the gifts
that we can give back to her.

Walters, Anna. *The Two-Legged Creature: An Otoe Story*. Northland
Publishing, 1993.
This Otoe Indian legend explains how, after a magically
harmonious period in the world when Man and the animals
lived in peace, Man changed and became abusive, so that
only Dog and Horse remained close.

RELATED POETRY

The Trees Stand Shining: Poetry of the North American Indians. New
York: Dial Books, 1993.

RELATED TEACHER RESOURCES

Caduto, Michael J. and Joseph Bruchac. *Keepers of the Earth: Native
American Stories and Environmental Activities for Children*. Fulcrum,
1989.

Carson, Rachel. *The Sense of Wonder*. Harper & Row, 1965.

Petrash, Carol. *Earthways: Simple Environmental Activities for Young
Children*. Gryphon House, 1992.

Rockwell, Robert and Robert Williams. *Hug a Tree & Other Things to
Do Outdoors with Young Children*. Gryphon House, 1983.

THE ENVIRONMENT

RELATED PICTURE BOOKS:

Baker, Jeannie. *Where the Forest Meets the Sea*. Greenwillow Books, 1987.

> On a camping trip in an Australian rain forest with his father, a young boy thinks about the history of the plant and animal life around him and wonders about their future.

Baker, Jeannie. *Window*. Greenwillow Books, 1991.

> Chronicles the events and changes in a young boy's life and in his environment, from babyhood to grownup, through wordless scenes observed from the window of his room.

Brown, Laurene. *Dinosaurs to the Rescue! A Guide to Protecting Our Planet*. Little, Brown, 1992.

> Text and illustrations of dinosaur characters introduce the earth's major environmental problems and suggest ways children can help.

Brown, Ruth. *The World That Jack Built*. Dutton Children's Books, 1991.

> In this variation of "The House That Jack Built" the cumulative text reveals that Jack's action of building a factory on his land has a damaging effect on his surroundings.

Bunting, Eve. *Someday a Tree*. Clarion Books, 1993.

> A young girl, her parents, and their neighbors try to save an old oak tree that has been poisoned by pollution.

Chen, Tony. *Run, Zebra, Run*. Lothrop, Lee & Shepard, 1972.

> Verses describe the wonders of the animal world and their impending destruction as a result of man's technological advances.

Cherry, Lynne. *The Great Kapok Tree*. Harcourt Brace Jovanovich, 1990.

> The many different animals that live in a great kapok tree in the Brazilian rainforest try to convince a man with an ax of the importance of not cutting down their home.

Cooney, Barbara. ***Miss Rumphius***. Viking Penguin, 1982.
Once long ago, Miss Rumphius was a little girl named Alice who lived by the sea. When she grew older, she remembered her grandfather's words: "You must do something to make the world more beautiful."

DePaola, Tomie. ***Michael Bird-Boy***. Prentice Hall, 1975.
A young boy who loves the countryside determines to find the source of the black cloud that hovers above it.

Geraghty, Paul. ***Stop That Noise***. Crown Publishing, 1992.
A tree mouse comes to appreciate the noises of the other forest animals after hearing the noise of a machine destroying the forest.

Gibbons, Gail. ***Recycle! A Handbook for Kids***. Little, Brown, 1992.
Explains the process of recycling from start to finish and discusses what happens to paper, glass, aluminum cans, and plastic when they are recycled into new products.

Glimmerveen, Ulco. ***A Tale of Antarctica***. Scholastic, 1989.
Uses a story of penguins in Antarctica to demonstrate how their environment is threatened by the pollution from man's presence.

Greene, Carol. ***The Old Ladies Who Liked Cats***. Harper & Row, 1991.
When the old ladies are no longer allowed to let their cats out at night, the delicate balance of their island ecology is disturbed, with disastrous results. Based on a story by Charles Darwin.

Heine, Helme. ***The Pearl***. Atheneum, 1985.
Beaver's excitement at finding a mussel that doubtless contains a pearl is tempered by the realization that such a treasure could stir the greed of his friends, causing a chain of environmentally disastrous events.

London, Jonathan. ***Voices of the Wild***. Crown Publishing, 1993.
Beaver, Bear, Deer, and other animals speak about their lives in the wild and their relationship with humans.

Luenn, Nancy. *Song for the Ancient Forest*. Atheneum, 1993.
Raven warns against the destruction of the ancient forests, but no one listens except for a small child.

Mendoza, George. *Were You a Wild Duck, Where Would You Go?* Stewart, Tabori & Chang, 1990.
A wild duck narrator looks at the past when the environment was bountiful, searches through today's polluted environment for a home, and encourages saving and restoring the environment for the future.

Norman, Lilith. *The Paddock: A Song in Praise of the Earth*. Alfred A. Knopf, 1992.
A patch of ground in Australia, formed millions of years ago, endures constant changes, outlasting the elements and the plants, animals, and people that come and go around it.

Peet, Bill. *The Wump World*. Houghton Mifflin, 1970.
The Wump World is an unspoiled place until huge monsters bring hordes of tiny creatures from the planet Pollutus.

Ray, Mary Lyn. *Pumpkins*. Harcourt Brace Jovanovich, 1992.
A man harvests and sells a bountiful crop of pumpkins so that he will be able to preserve a field from developers.

Seuss, Dr. *The Lorax*. Random House, 1971.
The Once-ler describes the results of the local pollution problem.

Shanks, Ann. *About Garbage and Stuff*. Viking Press, 1973.
Text and photographs introduce the reasons for and processes of recycling waste materials.

VanAllsburg, Chris. *Just a Dream*. Houghton Mifflin, 1990.
When he has a dream about a future Earth devastated by pollution, Walter begins to understand the importance of taking care of the environment.

GOING PLACES

RELATED PICTURE BOOKS

Baker, Leslie. **Morning Beach**. Little, Brown, 1990.
Relates a young girl's early morning trip to the ocean with her mother on the first day of summer vacation.

Barton, Byron. **Airport**. Crowell, 1982.
Describes and pictures what happens from the time an airplane passenger arrives at an airport, and boards an airplane until the plane is in the air.

Brown, Laura and Marc. **Dinosaurs Travel: A Guide for Families on the Go**. Joy Street Books, 1988.
Text and illustrations of dinosaur characters discuss the practicalities and pleasures of travel, from packing up and taking off to returning home again.

Brown, Ruth. **Our Puppy's Vacation**. Dutton, 1987.
It's puppy's first vacation, and everything is new and full of adventure. She bravely faces waves at the beach, climbs hills and walls, and makes some unexpected new friends.

Burningham, John. **Mr. Gumpy's Motor Car**. Crowell, 1976.
Mr. Gumpy's human and animal friends squash into his old car and go for a drive—until it starts to rain.

Burt, Denise. **Our Family Vacation**. G. Stevens, 1985.
Luis enjoys his vacation at the beach where he finds new ways of enjoying himself with his family and discovers a great many new things.

Chall, Marsha. **Up North at the Cabin**. Lothrop, Lee & Shepard, 1992.
Summer vacation up north at the cabin provides memorable experiences with the water, the animals, and other faces of nature.

Cowen-Fletcher, Jane. *Mama Zooms*. Scholastic, 1993.
   A boy's wonderful mama takes him zooming everywhere with her, because her wheelchair is a zooming machine.

Crews, Donald. *Flying*. Greenwillow Books, 1986.
   An airplane takes off, flies, and lands after having passed over cities, country areas, lakes, and more.

Crews, Donald. *Sail Away*. Greenwillow Books, 1995.
   A family takes an enjoyable trip in their sailboat and watches the weather change throughout the day.

Denslow, Sharon. *Riding with Aunt Lucy*. Bradbury Press, 1991.
   On drives with his friend Leonard's great-aunt, Walter never knows what the trio will discover.

Florian, Douglas. *A Beach Day*. Greenwillow Books, 1990.
   Describes simply how one family enjoys a day at the beach. Includes a list of seashells for which to look.

Gay, Michel. *Little Auto*. Macmillan, 1986.
   After a rocky start, little auto and a beach crab become friends and share the remainder of the day on the beach together.

Goodall, John. *An Edwardian Holiday*. Atheneum, 1979.
   A family visit to the seashore in Edwardian England.

Greenberg, Melanie. *At the Beach*. Dutton, 1989.
   Evokes the mood prevailing at the beach where the sun shines, seashells whisper, waves froth, and sand castles grow tall.

Hartman, Gail. *As the Crow Flies: A First Book of Maps*. Bradbury Press, 1991.
   A look at different geographical, areas from the perspectives of an eagle, rabbit, crow, horse and gull.

Howard, Elizabeth. ***The Train to Lulu's***. Bradbury Press, 1988.
The experiences of two young sisters traveling alone on the train to their grandmother's house.

Hudson, Wade. ***I Love My Family***. Scholastic, 1993.
At a joyous family reunion, relatives sing, dance, eat lots of food, and pose for a family picture.

Levinson, Riki. ***I Go with My Family to Grandma's***. Dutton, 1986.
As five cousins and their families arrive by various means of transportation, Grandma's home in Brooklyn gets livelier and livelier.

McPhail, David. ***Emma's Vacation***. E. P. Dutton, 1987.
Emma's idea of a good vacation is quite different from that of her parents.

McPhail, David. ***First Flight***. Little, Brown, 1987.
A naughty teddy bear, in contrast with his well-behaved owner, ignores all the rules and disrupts their first airplane trip.

Monfried, Lucia. ***The Daddies' Boat***. Dutton, 1990.
A child looks forward to the weekend when the boat brings her mother to their vacation home.

Morris, Ann. ***On the Go***. Lothrop, Lee & Shepard, 1990.
Discusses the ways in which people all over the world move from place to place, including walking, riding on animals, and traveling on wheels and water.

Oxenbury, Helen. ***The Car Trip***. E. P. Dutton, 1983.
A small boy's car trip with his parents turns out to be less than relaxing for his mother and father.

Rockwell, Anne. ***At the Beach***. Macmillan, 1987.
A child experiences enjoyable sights and sounds during a day at the beach.

Rockwell, Anne. *On Our Vacation*. Dutton, 1989.
    Throughout the Bear Family's summer vacation, objects and activities related to the setting are displayed for preschoolers' identification.

Rockwell, Anne. *Things That Go*. E. P. Dutton, 1986.
    Trains, tow trucks, sailboats, buses, sleds, jeeps, bicycles, and other things that go can be seen in the city, in the country, on the water, in the park, and many other places.

Roffey, Maureen. *I Spy on Vacation*. Four Winds Press, 1988.
    Readers may finish sentences by saying what they "spy" in pictures of a beach vacation.

Rylant, Cynthia. *The Relatives Came*. Bradbury Press, 1985.
    The relatives come to visit from Virginia and everyone has a wonderful time.

SUMMER

Farmer's Market

Objectives
- Children's natural senses of wonder will be enhanced.
- Children will learn where many foods come from.
- Children will learn which vegetables grow under and which grow above the ground
- Children will learn which parts of plants are edible.

COMMENTARY

Summer Theme

Farmer's Market provides a flexible theme for a summer session. It encompasses not only gardening projects but also a general theme of "where food comes from." You may wish to include field trips to dairy farms, orchards, or other places where food is grown or distributed.

It is important that children grow up feeling they are a part of the natural world. Eating food that children have grown themselves provides an invaluable opportunity to sense the interconnectedness of all things. Children may prepare the soil, plant the seeds, and nurture the growing plants as they reach maturity. They may observe close-up the effects of weather, insects, and animals on the plants. When the time comes to harvest food from the living plants, children can feel gratitude for the gift of food that plants provide.

Many children are more likely to try eating various kinds of vegetables when they have helped grow them. Children's self-esteem may also be enhanced by taking responsibility for the tending of a garden.

Help children "examine" the vegetables, inside and outside, using all five senses (see page 228). *Growing Colors* by Bruce McMillan is a good book to share with children during the summer. You may also wish to refer to *Creative Food Experiences for Children* by Mary T. Goodwin and Gerry Pollen (Center for Science in the Public Interest, 1980.)

Dear Family:

Our summer theme is **Farmer's Market**. We have posted a sign-up sheet at school that lists a variety of fruits and vegetables. Your child may bring in something on the list or share something unusual. We encourage you to send produce from your own garden or from a farmer's market whenever possible. In addition, we would appreciate a snack for the class that features the particular vegetable or fruit your child chooses to share. Your child may talk about the produce and how it grows at sharing time. Together, we will examine the fruit or vegetable using our five senses. First, we will examine the outside of the fruit or vegetable. Then we will cut it open carefully and look at the inside.

Children will learn how foods grow (above or below the ground) and which parts of plants are edible. We will take trips to a dairy farm or pick-it-yourself orchard and we might even develop our own "green thumbs!"

Sincerely,

Your Child's Teachers

FARMER'S MARKET

COOKING PROJECTS

Ladybug Salads

You will need lettuce leaves, tomatoes (cut in half), black olives, and raisins for this salad, as well as small paper plates. Invite each child to place a tomato half flat-side down on a lettuce leaf, which in turn has been placed on a paper plate. This is the ladybug's body. Have them place black olives where the heads would be and arrange five or six raisins on the "backs" of the tomatoes for spots. Tiny olive slices may be added for legs as well. Sprinkle with salt or dressing and enjoy!

Cucumber-pillars

You will need sliced cucumbers, carrots, or celery cut into small, matchstick shapes, raisins, and ranch dressing or dip for this salad, as well as small paper plates and plastic knives. Have children spread a bit of dressing or dip on four or five cucumber slices and arrange the slices in an overlapping line on paper plates. This will be the cucumber-pillar's body. Carrot or celery sticks may be added for legs and feelers and raisins for eyes. Sprinkle with salt and pepper if desired and dig in!

ARTS & CRAFTS PROJECTS

Fruit or Veggie T-Shirts

Have children bring in clean, white or light-colored T-shirts from home for this project. Invite children to choose a favorite fruit or vegetable to draw in pencil. Once they are satisfied with their drawings, help children redraw their fruits or vegetables on clean, white paper with iron-on crayons. Be sure they press down on the crayons for vivid colors. Invite parent volunteers to help pin the crayon drawings face-down on the T-shirts and transfer with a heated iron according to crayon directions. When shirts have cooled, they are ready to be worn or sent home.

Sponge Paintings

Cut a number of sponges into fruit and vegetable shapes, such as an apple, an orange, a banana, a cucumber, a carrot, and a squash. Pour tempera paints of appropriate colors into small bowls and show children how they can create interesting designs on colored construction paper by dipping the sponges into the paint and then onto the paper. If you prefer, children may sponge-paint plain shoe boxes to use as treasure boxes at home.

RELATED SONGS

Ol' Peter Rabbit

Mississippi Folk Song

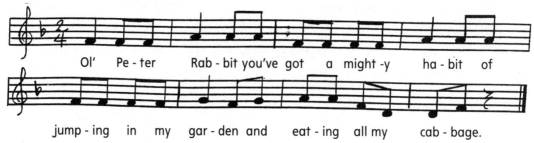

Ol' Pe-ter Rab-bit you've got a might-y ha-bit of

jump-ing in my gar-den and eat-ing all my cab-bage.

Game

Play a game similar to "London Bridge." Invite children to walk under two children's upraised arms. Children try to keep from getting trapped on the word *cabbage*. Can children think of other vegetables the rabbit might eat?

Rabbit, rabbit, carrot-eater
Says he, "There is nothing sweeter
Than a carrot every day."
Munch and crunch and run away.

– Anonymous

FEATURED BOOK

Potter, Beatrix. ***The Tale of Peter Rabbit***. Warne, 1993.

Mrs. Rabbit told her children *not* to go into Mr. McGregor's garden. Flopsy, Mopsy, and Cottontail were good little bunnies, but Peter, who was very naughty, got into trouble.

FARMER'S MARKET

RELATED SONGS

Green Peas
Tune of the Civil War, "Goober Peas"

Peas! Peas! Peas! Peas! Eat - ing green peas!

Good - ness how de - li - cious, eat - ing green peas!

Round and round the cornfield
Looking for a hare.
Where can we find one?
Right up there!

— Traditional

While chanting the rhyme, hold up the child's palm, to trace circles upon it. On "right up there," run fingers under the arm to give a tickle.

FEATURED BOOK

Wilson, Sarah. ***Muskrat, Muskrat, Eat Your Peas***. Simon & Schuster, 1989.

After Muskrat's family meticulously plants, waters, and harvests peas, Muskrat doesn't want any.

RELATED SONGS

Oats, Peas, Beans and Barley Grow

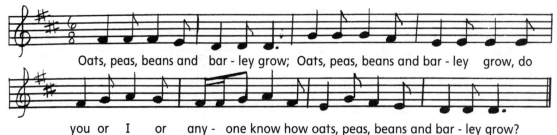

Oats, peas, beans and bar - ley grow; Oats, peas, beans and bar - ley grow, do

you or I or any - one know how oats, peas, beans and bar - ley grow?

(Chorus)

1. First the farmer sows his seed, *(throws out seed)*
   Then he stands and takes his ease, *(folds arms)*
   Stamps his foot and claps his hands, *(stamps, claps)*
   And turns around to view the land. *(farmer shades his eyes)*

(Chorus)

2. Waiting for a partner,
   Waiting for a partner,
   Open the ring and take one in,
   While all the others dance and sing.
   (The "farmer" chooses another child to be the next farmer)

(Chorus)

3. Tra la la la la la, etc.

Actions

Invite children to stand in a circle, holding hands. One child, the "farmer," stands in the center. Children circle around the farmer during the chorus. With each verse, the "farmer" performs the motions indicated as children sing.

Chop, chop, choppity-chop.
Cut off the bottom,
And cut off the top.

What there is left we will
Put in the pot;
Chop, chop, choppity-chop.

– Anonymous

FARMER'S MARKET

RELATED PICTURE BOOKS

Briggs, Raymond. *Jim and the Beanstalk*. Coward-McCann, 1970.
An updated version of the well-known tale. Jim climbs the beanstalk and discovers a toothless old giant who can no longer eat little boys.

Butterworth, Nick and Mick Inkpen. *Jasper's Beanstalk*. Bradbury Press, 1993.
Jasper hopes to grow a beanstalk, but becomes discouraged when the bean he plants doesn't grow after a week.

Caseley, Judith. *Grandpa's Garden Lunch*. Greenwillow Books, 1990.
After helping Grandpa in the garden, Sarah and her grandparents enjoy a lunch made with homegrown vegetables.

Demarest, Chris. *No Peas for Nellie*. Macmillan, 1988.
Nellie imagines all the things she would rather eat than her peas, and while doing so she finishes them all.

Demi. *The Empty Pot*. Henry Holt, 1990.
When Ping admits that he is the only child in China unable to grow a flower from the seeds distributed by the Emperor, he is rewarded for his honesty.

Ehlert, Lois. *Eating the Alphabet: Fruits and Vegetables from A to Z*. Harcourt Brace Jovanovich, 1989.
An alphabetical tour of the world of fruits and vegetables, from apricots and artichokes to yams and zucchini.

Ehlert, Lois. *Planting a Rainbow*. Harcourt Brace Jovanovich, 1988.
A mother and daughter plant a rainbow of flowers in the family garden.

Florian, Douglas. *Vegetable Garden*. Harcourt Brace Jovanovich, 1991.
A family plants a vegetable garden and helps it grow to a rich harvest.

Howe, John. *Jack and the Beanstalk*. Little, Brown, 1989.
A boy climbs to the top of a giant beanstalk where he uses his quick wits to outsmart a giant and make his and his mother's fortune.

Hurd, Thatcher. *The Pea Patch Jig*. Crown Publishing, 1986.
The adventures of Baby Mouse who loves to go exploring in the garden. Despite being picked with the lettuce and almost ending up in a salad, Baby Mouse refuses to stay out of Farmer Clem's garden.

Koscielniak, Bruce. *Bear and Bunny Grow Tomatoes*. Alfred A. Knopf, 1993.
A hard working bear and a lazy bunny both plant tomatoes in their gardens, with quite different results.

LeTord, Bijou. *Rabbit Seeds*. Four Winds Press, 1984.
A gardener's work begins in spring when the sun warms up the earth and ends when leaves turn yellow in autumn.

McMillan, Bruce. *Growing Colors*. Lothrop, Lee & Shepard, 1988.
Photographs of green peas, yellow corn, red potatoes, purple beans, and other fruits and vegetables illustrate the many colors of nature.

Oechsli, Helen and Kelly. *In My Garden: A Child's Gardening Book*. Macmillan, 1985.
A general guide to beginning gardening, with specific instructions for growing beans, carrots, lettuce, peppers, and other vegetables.

Potter, Beatrix. *The Tale of Peter Rabbit*. Frederick Warne, 1993.
Mrs. Rabbit told her children NOT to go into Mr. McGregor's garden. Flopsy, Mopsy and Cottontail were good little bunnies, but Peter, who was very naughty, got into trouble.

Ryder, Joanne. ***Dancers in the Garden***. Sierra Book Club, 1992.
Follows the activities of a hummingbird and his mate in a
garden on a sunny day.

Rylant, Cynthia. ***This Year's Garden***. Bradbury Press, 1984.
Follows the seasons of the year as reflected in the growth,
life, and death of the garden of a large rural family.

Titherington, Jeanne. ***Pumpkin, Pumpkin***. Greenwillow Books, 1986.
Jamie plants a pumpkin seed and, after watching it grow,
carves it, and saves some seeds to plant in the spring.

Wallis, Diz. ***Something Nasty in the Cabbages***. Caroline House, 1991.
A retold tale of Chanticleer and Reynard the fox, beautifully
illustrated.

Wilkes, Angela. ***My First Garden Book***. Alfred A. Knopf, 1992.
Features simple gardening projects from collecting seeds to
growing a miniature desert garden.

Wilner, Isabel. ***A Garden Alphabet***. Dutton Children's Books, 1991.
Rhyming verses and illustrations introduce the letters of the
alphabet and describe how a garden is planned and
planted, how things grow, and the joy a garden brings.

Wilson, Sarah. ***Muskrat, Muskrat, Eat Your Peas!*** Simon & Schuster,
1989.
After Muskrat's family meticulously plants, waters, and
harvests peas, Muskrat doesn't want any.

Dear Family:

We look forward to celebrating children's birthdays at school. Your child will have a designated sharing day as close to his or her birthday as possible. Summer birthdays will be observed in either September or May. In addition to bringing sharing items for the monthly theme, your child may also bring a special birthday sharing. We would all enjoy seeing photographs of your child taken over the years. Perhaps the photographs can be made into a timeline poster or a little book. A special piece of your child's baby clothing would illustrate how much your child has grown!

We suggest you send birthday muffins as a special treat for the class—we've included a recipe you may wish to try.

Sincerely,

Your Child's Teachers

Applesauce Muffins

2 1/2 cups whole wheat flour	2 eggs
4 tsp. baking powder	2 cups applesauce
1 1/2 tsp. cinnamon	1 cup honey
1/2 tsp. salt	2/3 cup vegetable oil
1/2 tsp. ginger	2 cups raisins

Preheat oven to 350°. Combine dry and wet ingredients separately, then stir together until just moist. Spoon into paper muffin cups. Bake muffins for about 25 minutes. This recipe makes approximately two dozen muffins.

Mexican Birthday Song

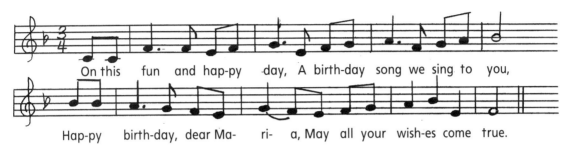

On this fun and hap-py day, A birth-day song we sing to you,

Hap-py birth-day, dear Ma- ri- a, May all your wish-es come true.

Birthday Chant
Apples, peaches, pears and plums,
Tell me when your birthday comes.
January, February, March, April . . .

Encourage children to clap in rhythm, stopping on the month of the child's birthday. This rhyme could also be used for jumping rope or ball bouncing.

BIRTHDAY TIME

RELATED PICTURE BOOKS

Aliki. *June 7!* Macmillan, 1972.
> Just as a young girl and her family sit down to lunch, the doorbell rings. Relatives of varying degrees continue pouring into the apartment until it becomes necessary for them all to go to the park where they celebrate the girl's birthday.

Anholt, Catherine. *The Snow Fairy and the Spaceman*. Delacorte, 1991.
> One of the costumed guests at a birthday party is not enjoying himself at all, until he has a chance to help out the birthday girl.

Asch, Frank. *Happy Birthday, Moon*. Prentice, 1982.
> When a bear discovers that the moon shares his birthday, he buys the moon a beautiful hat as a present.

Barrett, Judi. *Benjamin's 365 Birthdays*. Aladdin Books, 1992.
> Benjamin figures out how to have a birthday every day of the year.

Base, Graeme. *The Eleventh Hour: A Curious Mystery*. Harry N. Abrams, 1989.
> An elephant's eleventh birthday party is marked by eleven games preceding the banquet to be eaten at the eleventh hour, but when the time to eat arrives, the birthday feast has disappeared. The reader is invited to guess the thief.

Brandenberg, Franz. *Aunt Nina and Her Nephews and Nieces*. Greenwillow Books, 1983.
> When Aunt Nina gives a birthday party for her cat, the guests receive surprise presents.

Brown, Marc. *The Cloud Over Clarence*. Dutton, 1979.
> A special birthday present helps Clarence rid his days of accidents and forgetfulness.

Bunting, Eve. ***Happy Birthday, Dear Duck***. Clarion Books, 1988.
Duck's birthday gifts from his animal friends are wonderful but cannot be used away from water, a problem solved by the last gift.

Burton, Marilee. ***Oliver's Birthday***. Harper, 1986.
Oliver the ostrich is convinced that his friends have forgotten his birthday when no one seems to come to help him celebrate.

Carlstrom, Nancy White. ***Happy Birthday, Jesse Bear!*** Macmillan, 1994.
Rhyming text and illustrations describe all the activities associated with Jesse Bear's birthday.

Caseley, Judith. ***Three Happy Birthdays***. Greenwillow Books, 1989.
Chronicles the birthday celebrations of three family members and what they do with their favorite birthday gifts.

Duncan, Lois. ***Birthday Moon***. Viking, 1989.
Relates the wonderful things you can do with the perfect birthday gift—the moon.

Goennel, Heidi. ***It's My Birthday***. Tambourine Books, 1992.
A child celebrates a birthday with a party, long-distance telephone call, special card, cake and gifts.

Hurd, Thatcher. ***Little Mouse's Birthday Cake***. HarperCollins, 1992.
Disappointed that his friends seem to have forgotten his birthday, Little Mouse goes skiing by himself.

Hutchins. ***Happy Birthday, Sam***. Greenwillow Books, 1978.
Sam's birthday brings a solution to several of his problems.

Inkpen, Mick. ***Kipper's Birthday***. Harcourt Brace Jovanovich, 1993.
A delay in delivering the invitations to Kipper the dog's birthday party causes his friends to come on the wrong day.

Ketteman, Helen. ***Not Yet, Yvette***. Albert Whitman, 1992.
A girl waits impatiently as she and her father prepare a surprise birthday party for her mother.

Krauss, Ruth. ***The Birthday Party***. Harper & Row, 1957.
A boy, David, who had been everywhere but to a birthday party gets a surprise.

Limmer, Milly. ***Where Do Little Girls Grow?*** Albert Whitman, 1993.
A mother and a daughter imagine several possibilities as to where the little girl came from and then describe how she was actually born.

Miller, Margaret. ***My Birthday Party***. HarperCollins, 1991.
Labeled photos present words associated with birthday parties, such as *friends, cake, sing,* and *open*.

Oppenheim, Shulamith. ***Waiting for Noah***. HarperCollins, 1990.
Noah hears the story of the day that his grandmother waited for him to be born.

Peck, Mere. ***Mary Wore Her Red Dress and Henry Wore His Green Sneakers***. Clarion Books, 1985.
Adapted from the Texas folk song. Each of Katy's animal friends wears a different color of clothing to her birthday party.

Rice, Eve. ***Benny Bakes a Cake***. Greenwillow Books, 1993.
When the dog eats Benny's birthday cake, Daddy comes to the rescue.

Rylant, Cynthia. ***Birthday Presents***. Orchard Books, 1987.
A five-year-old girl listens as her mother and father describe her four previous birthday celebrations.

Schweninger, Ann. ***Birthday Wishes***. Viking Kestrel, 1986.
The Rabbit family's festivities for Buttercup's fifth birthday make all her wishes come true.

Waber, Bernard. *Lyle and the Birthday Party*. Houghton Mifflin, 1966.
Lyle, the lovable crocodile, becomes mean green jealous as everyone makes preparations for Joshua's birthday party.

Yolen, Jane. *Mouse's Birthday*. G.P. Putnam's Sons, 1993.
One after another, several animals try to squeeze into Mouse's house to help him celebrate his birthday.

Yolen, Jane. *Picnic with Piggins*. Harcourt Brace Jovanovich, 1988.
A picnic in the country develops a mystery which turns out to be a birthday surprise.

EXPLORING FRUIT USING THE FIVE SENSES

Sometimes children will be asked to bring in particular fruits. Examples of questions to ask to heighten children's sensory awareness follow.

EXAMINING AN APPLE

OUTSIDE (Display different varieties.)

Sight
How many different kinds of apples do you see? Do you know the names for the different kinds? What different colors do you see? How many different sizes do you see? How do their shapes differ? Can you tell which side of the apple was facing the sun? Is it round or dimpled where the stem comes out?

Touch
Is the skin smooth or bumpy? Is the apple hard or soft? Does your apple have any soft spots or bruises?

Smell
Do you smell your apple? What words describe the smell?

Sound
What sound does your apple make when you roll it? Tap on it? Eat it?

INSIDE (Cut apples in half—some crosswise, some lengthwise.)

Sight
Crosswise: *Can you find the star inside your apple? How many seeds can you count? What color are the seeds? Are they the same color all the way through?*
Lengthwise: *What shape is your apple now? Can you find the outline of the core?*

Touch
When you take a bite of your apple, does it feel crisp or soft? Is it wet or dry? Can you squeeze it to make juice?

Smell
Does the inside of your apple smell the same as the outside? Do you like its smell?

Sound
How can you make a crunching noise with your apple? Do you hear the apple when it is being cut?

Taste
Is your apple sweet or is it tart? What are some ways to eat apples?

EXAMINING AN ORANGE

OUTSIDE (Compare juice oranges, navel oranges, tangerines.)

Sight
How do you think oranges got their name? What shape is an orange? Where was the orange's stem?

Touch
Is the peel smooth or bumpy? Is an orange soft or hard? Can you squeeze it?

Smell
With your eyes closed, can you tell which is a ball and which is the orange?

Sound
How can you make your orange make a noise? Do you hear it when you shake it? Roll it? Squeeze it?

INSIDE (Some should be peeled. Cut some in half crosswise, some lengthwise.)

Sight
Crosswise: *What colors do you see? What does the inside look like? How many seeds can you find?*
Lengthwise: *Can you find the smile shape?*
Peeled oranges: *What color is the inside of the peel?*
Does the inside of the orange have a membrane? What color is it? What does it look like when you peel some off the orange? Is everybody's peel the same thickness?

Touch
Is the orange wet or dry inside? Can you squeeze any juice? Are the seeds hard or soft?

Smell
Smell the inside of the orange. (Show children how to fold a piece of orange peel to make a thin spray.) *Smell your fingers. How do they smell?*

Sound
What words might describe the sound of an orange being juiced? Being peeled?

Taste
Is it sweet or sour? What foods are made from oranges? Have you ever had marmalade on toast? How did it taste? How does the peel taste?

EXAMINING A BANANA

OUTSIDE (Display bananas in varying degrees of ripeness.)

Sight

Look at all the bananas that have been brought to school. What color are they? How can you tell when a banana is ripe? What color are unripe bananas? How do bananas look when they are still on the tree? Are all the bananas the same size?

Touch

How does a banana feel? Is it warm or cold? Is it hard or soft? Can you make a mark on the peel?

Smell

Does the banana have an aroma? Do all the bananas smell the same? Which ones have a stronger aroma?

Sound

Is there any way you could make a sound with your banana? Let's peel it now and listen to the sound.

INSIDE

Sight

What color is the inside of the banana? What color is the inside of the peel? Find the seeds. Do the seeds make a pattern?

Touch

Touch the inside of the peel. Is it wet or dry? How does it feel? What does the banana feel like? Is it soft or hard? Why do you think mothers give bananas to babies for their first food?

Smell

Does the banana smell the same as it did before it was peeled? Smell your fingers. Do you like the smell of bananas?

Sound

Does the banana make a noise when you eat it? Does it crunch like an apple when you eat it? Does it make a quiet sound?

Taste

How would you describe the special taste of bananas? What other ways do you eat bananas? How does banana feel on your tongue? Does it stick to your teeth?

FRUIT FUN
RELATED SONG

Tarzan of the Apes
Tune, "John Brown's Body"

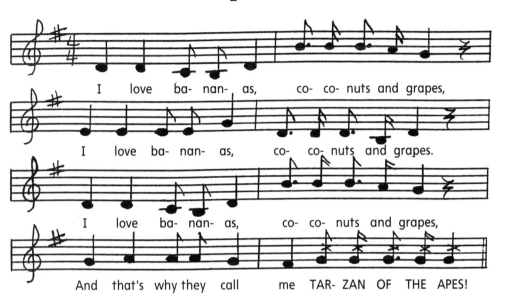

I love ba-nan-as, co-co-nuts and grapes,
I love ba-nan-as, co-co-nuts and grapes.
I love ba-nan-as, co-co-nuts and grapes,
And that's why they call me TAR-ZAN OF THE APES!

If I were an apple
And grew on a tree
I think I'd drop down
On a nice boy like me.
I wouldn't stay there
Giving nobody joy,
I'd fall down at once
And say, "Eat me, my boy!"

– Mother Goose

Away up high in the apple tree
(hold arms over head)
Two red apples smiled at me.
(form circles with fingers of both hands)
I shook that tree as hard as I could.
(grasp hands together and shake)
Down came the apples,
(move hands down)
And mmmm, were they good!
(rub stomach)

FRUIT FUN

RELATED PICTURE BOOKS

Bang, Molly. *The Grey Lady and the Strawberry Snatcher*. Four Winds Press, 1984.
> A magical wordless fantasy that follows the Grey Lady's clever and surprising methods of eluding the Strawberry Snatcher, who is always close.

Bruchac, Joseph. *The First Strawberries: A Cherokee Story*. Dial Books, 1993.
> A quarrel between the first man and the first woman is reconciled when the Sun causes strawberries to grow out of the earth.

Carle, Eric. *The Very Hungry Caterpillar*. Philomel Books, 1979.
> Follows the progress of a hungry little caterpillar who eats his way through a varied and very large quantity of food until, full at last, he forms a cocoon around himself and goes to sleep.

Coldrey, Jennifer. *Strawberry*. Silver Burdett Press, 1988.
> Photographs, drawings, and text on two levels of difficulty describe how the strawberry plant produces juicy strawberries and sends out runners to start new plants.

Degen, Bruce. *Jamberry*. Harper & Row, 1983.
> A little boy walking in the forest meets a big lovable bear that takes him on a delicious berry picking adventure.

Fleming, Denise. *Lunch*. Henry Holt, 1992.
> A very hungry mouse eats a large lunch comprised of colorful fruits and vegetables.

Gibbons, Gail. *The Seasons of Arnold's Apple Tree*. Harcourt Brace Jovanovich, 1984.
> As the seasons pass, Arnold enjoys a variety of activities as a result of his apple tree. Includes a recipe for apple pie and a description of how an apple cider press works.

Hogrogian, Nonny. **Apples**. Macmillan, 1972.
    The apple peddler replenishes his cart from the trees that grow from the discarded cores of the apples he sells.

Lapp, Eleanor. **The Blueberry Bears**. Albert Whitman, 1983.
    Hungry bears invade Bessie Allen's cabin after she picks clean the blueberry patch in the woods and stockpiles the berries in her kitchen.

McCloskey, Robert. **Blueberries for Sal**. Viking Penguin, 1948.
    Little Sal and Little Bear both lose their mothers while eating blueberries and almost end up with the other's mother.

Mitgutsch, Ali. **From Seed to Pear**. Carolrhoda Books, 1971.
    Describes the cycle of a pear seed which, when planted, produces a fruit-bearing tree and a new supply of new seeds.

Orbach, Ruth. **Apple Pigs**. W. Collins & World Publishing, 1977.
    A family suddenly inundated with apples from a once dried-up tree finds a very enjoyable way to dispose of the surplus.

Polushkin, Maria. **Mama's Secret**. Four Winds Press, 1984.
    When Mama tiptoes out of the house, Amy, Baby and Kitty tiptoe after her to find out her delicious secret.

Rockwell, Anne. **Apples and Pumpkins**. Macmillan, 1989.
    In preparation for Halloween night, a family visits Mr. Comstock's farm to pick apples and pumpkins.

Watts, Barrie. **Apple Tree**. Silver Burdett Press, 1987.
    Describes in simple text and photographs how an apple develops from a blossom in the spring to a ripe fruit in the autumn.

ARTS & CRAFTS RECIPES

Play Dough
1 cup white flour
1/4 cup salt
2 Tbsp. cream of tartar
1 cup water
2 tsp. food coloring
1 Tbsp. vegetable oil

Mix dry ingredients in a medium pot. Combine and add wet ingredients. Cook over medium heat and stir until dough forms a big lump. Knead on a lightly floured surface. Store in an airtight container.

Baker's Clay
1 cup salt
4 cups flour
1 1/2 cup water
1/3 to 1/2 cup liquid tempera (optional)

Mix ingredients thoroughly by hand, adding more water if necessary. Knead about five minutes or until dough is soft and pliable. Do not mix ahead of time, as clay loses malleability the longer it is stored and becomes too sticky. Items made from uncolored dough may be baked in a slow oven. Items made with colored dough should be air-dried.

Basic Clay
1 cup cornstarch
2 cups baking soda
1 1/4 cups water
food coloring (optional)

Combine ingredients. Cook and stir over medium heat until very thick. Place mixture on a piece of aluminum foil to knead. Store in refrigerator.

Salt Ceramic
1 cup salt
1/2 cup cornstarch
3/4 cup water

Put ingredients in a cooking pot and stir constantly over medium heat. When mixture thickens into a big lump, place on aluminum foil to knead. Let items air-dry. Small objects, such as cloves, feathers, or wire hanging loops, may be embedded while salt ceramic is still soft. When dried to rock hardness, objects may be preserved with clear glaze.

Quick Fingerpaint Recipe #1

Sprinkle tempera paint or food coloring over liquid starch or non-detergent liquid soap.

Fingerpaint Recipe #2

4 cups water
1 cup flour
1 Tbsp. alum
food coloring

While putting three cups of water on to boil, mix one one cup of flour with one cup of cold water and stir until smooth. Add to boiling water. Cook and stir. Add alum and food coloring.

Bubble Mixture

2 cups Joy™ detergent
6 cups water
3/4 cup corn syrup

This recipe works well for both big and small bubbles. Cans open at both ends may be used as wands. Empty thread spools make great wands for small bubbles.

Cinnamon Ornaments

1 1/2 cups ground cinnamon
1 cup applesauce

Mix cinnamon and applesauce together. Roll mixture between sheets of waxed paper to 1/4" (6.25 mm) thickness. Cut with cookie cutters. Air-dry on waxed paper overnight.

RECOMMENDED RESOURCE BOOKS

Herberholz, Barbara. *Early Childhood Art*. Wm. C. Brown, 1979.

Lasky, Lila and Rose Mukerji. *Art: Basic for Young Children*. NAEYC, 1980.

INDEX OF SONGS

Ring Out the Old, Ring In the New!
New Year Bells
The Grand Old Duke of York
Looby Loo
Jack Be Nimble
Deedle, Deedle Dumpling
Pease Porridge Hot
Open, Shut Them
Bounce High, Bounce Low

February:

Friendship Patchwork
The More We Are Together
A Tisket, A Tasket
Love Somebody
Skidamarink
Little Sally Waters
Ida Red
Old Brass Wagon

Animals Are Our Friends
The North Wind Doth Blow
Wild Bird
I Love Little Pussy
Rover
Nibble, Nibble, Nibble

March:

Hats, Hats, Hats
Mexican Hat Dance

Tickling Our Funny Bones
St. Patrick's Day
Aiken Drum
Hey Diddle Diddle

April:

Mother Goose on the Loose
Rain on the Green Grass
It's Raining, It's Pouring
Rain, Rain, Go Away
Mary Had a Little Lamb
Hot Cross Buns

Little Things
The Eency, Weency Spider
Six Little Ducks
Over in the Meadow
I Know a Little Pussy
Little Green Frog

May: **The Earth Is Our Mother**
Dance in the Circle
Under the Maypole
A Tribute to Old Friends
The Earth Is Our Mother

Going Places
We Go Traveling
Goodbye Song
Riding in a Car

Summer: **Farmer's Market**
Ol' Peter Rabbit
Green Peas
Oats, Peas, Beans and Barley Grow

Birthday Time: Mexican Birthday Song

Fruit Fun: Tarzan of the Apes

INDEX OF RECIPES

TEACHER NOTES